Praise for *Winners Never Cheat*

"How timely! How needed it is for one of the finest human beings, industrial leaders, and philanthropists on the planet to compellingly drill down on timeless, universal values for business and life. This book edifies, inspires, and motivates all of us to model these common sensical lessons for our organizations, all our relationships, and especially our posterity—for what is common sense is obviously not common practice.

Primary greatness is character and contribution. Secondary greatness is how most people define success—wealth, fame, position, etc. Few have both. Jon's one of them."

> —Dr. Stephen R. Covey, author, *The 7 Habits of Highly Effective People* and *The 8th Habit: From Effectiveness to Greatness*

"In his creative gifts, in his business success, in his great philanthropy, in his human qualities, Jon Huntsman stands in a class all of his own."

> —Richard Cheney, Vice President of the United States, on the occasion of the dedication of Huntsman Hall, The Wharton School, The University of Pennsylvania

"Jon Huntsman has successfully navigated corporate America guided by a strong moral compass. In his book, Jon shares his depth of knowledge and outlines how to succeed in today's competitive market place while taking the high ground."

> —Senator Elizabeth Dole

"Jon Huntsman's new book ought to be mandatory reading for leaders—and those who aspire to be leaders—in every field. His secrets for success are no secrets at all, but invaluable lessons that he has reminded us, with his life and now with his words, are the pillars upon which we can build our lives, too."

> —Senator Tom Daschle

"Jon Huntsman's book is about ethics, values, and his experiences. The practical way in which he shares those with the reader is amazing. This is a book with inspiration for a younger generation."

> —Jeroen van der Veer, Chief Executive, Royal Dutch/Shell Group

"As I read Jon's book, I thought my father had returned to tell me that you are either honest or you are dishonest, that there is nothing in between. 2 + 2 = 4, never 3.999 or 4.001. Also, if you always say what you believe, you don't need to have a good memory. If we could only live the principles Jon has followed, what a different world it would be—both in our business and personal relationships."

—Former U.S. Senator and Astronaut Jake Garn

"Jon Huntsman has taken us back to the basics—the basic values that transcend all professions and cultures. He has provided real-life examples that are inspiring and show that 'good guys' really can finish first. And he shows us how you can learn from mistakes. It is a 'must read' for both young men and women just stepping onto the golden escalator to success and anyone seeking reassurance that how one lives every day really does matter."

—Marsha J. Evans, former President and CEO, American Red Cross

"A refreshing and candid discussion on basic values that can guide you from the sandbox to the boardroom—told by a straight shooter."

—Chuck Prince, Chairman and CEO, Citigroup

"Jon's outlook on moral and ethical behavior in business should be inspirational to all who read this book. The lessons of fair play and holding true to personal moral values and ethics are time-honored principals which are all too often overlooked in today's world. While this book is geared to those in business, I see it as worthwhile reading to anyone."

—Rick Majerus, former ESPN Basketball Analyst and legendary basketball coach, St. Louis University.

"It is true that all business enterprises are profit oriented, but the avarice for wealth and the ardent desire to stay competitive tend to lure more and more corporate executives to resort to unscrupulous, unethical practices. Although they may achieve temporary successes, their lucrative lies and fraud will be their ultimate undoing, causing great losses to their shareholders. Jon's book is a stentorian call for the corporate world to reassert accepted moral values and learn the responsibility of sharing gains with society, probably in line with the economic standard of the country."

—Jeffrey L.S. Koo, Chairman and CEO, Chinatrust Financial Holding Co.

"Succinctly capturing what the world's major beliefs all hold as an unassailable truth, that ethical behavior and giving more than you receive is the path to fulfillment and success in life, *Winners Never Cheat* deftly navigates these concepts with clarity and insight."

—Louis Columbus, Director of Business Development, Cincom Systems

"This is easily the most courageous and personal business book since Bill George's *Authentic Leadership*. If anyone has doubts about how one person can make a substantive difference in the world, this beautifully written book should dispel them immediately. I hope its message is embraced worldwide."

—Charles Decker, Author of *Lessons from the Hive: The Buzz for Surviving and Thriving in an Ever-Changing Workplace*

"Jon Huntsman and I have this much in common: We were raised to work hard, play fair, keep your word, and give back to the community. I relate to what he is saying. Real winners never cheat."

—Karl Malone, Twice MVP of the NBA and Utah Jazz legend

"In an age of corporate scandal and excess, Jon Huntsman reminds us of the enduring value of honesty and respect. He shows us that morality and compassion are essential ingredients to true success. Over the years, Jon's extraordinary business achievements have been matched by a sense of charity that continues to touch countless lives. I am privileged to call him a friend."

—Mitt Romney, former Governor of Massachusetts

"I can't put down the book after reading the first page. These are values universally cherished, whether in the United States, in China, or elsewhere. A great and loving man emerges from the pages so vivid that he seems to talk to you face to face, like a family member. My life is richer and mind is broader after reading the book. I am very proud of my friendship with Jon Huntsman."

—Yafei He, Director General, Ministry of Foreign Affairs—China, Dept. of North American and Oceanic Affairs

"Nothing could be more timely than this provocative book from one of America's foremost business and civic leaders about the urgent need for greater ethics in our public and private lives. With wit and clarity, Jon Huntsman shares his guidelines for living a life of integrity and courage. It is a wonderful tonic for much of what ails us today. *Winners Never Cheat* is a valuable handbook for anyone wanting to succeed in business, or life."

—Andrea Mitchell, NBC News

"Jon Huntsman is more than a phenomenally successful entrepreneur. He is a giant of a leader and a role model of integrity. In *Winners Never Cheat: Everyday Values We Learned as Children (But May Have Forgotten)*, Mr. Huntsman establishes the inextricable link between following one's inner moral compass and achieving lasting success. His book is filled with timeless wisdom, timely examples, and an inspiring life story. Jon is the quintessential nice guy who has finished first!"

—Dr. Amy Gutmann, President, University of Pennsylvania

WINNERS
NEVER
CHEAT

WINNERS
NEVER
CHEAT

EVEN IN DIFFICULT TIMES

Jon M. Huntsman

Vice President, Publisher: Tim Moore
Associate Publisher and Director of Marketing: Amy Neidlinger
Editorial Assistant: Pamela Boland
Operations Manager: Gina Kanouse
Digital Marketing Manager: Julie Phifer
Publicity Manager: Laura Czaja
Assistant Marketing Manager: Megan Colvin
Cover Designer: Chuti Prasertsith
Managing Editor: Kristy Hart
Senior Project Editor: Lori Lyons
Copy Editor: Water Crest Publishing
Proofreader: San Dee Phillips
Interior Designer and Compositor: Gloria Schurick
Manufacturing Buyer: Dan Uhrig

Prentice Hall offers excellent discounts on this book when ordered in quantity
for bulk purchases or special sales. For more information, please contact U.S.
Corporate and Government Sales, 1-800-382-3419,
corpsales@pearsontechgroup.com. For sales outside the U.S., please contact
International Sales at international@pearson.com.

Pearson Education LTD.
Pearson Education Australia PTY, Limited.
Pearson Education Singapore, Pte. Ltd.
Pearson Education North Asia, Ltd.
Pearson Education Canada, Ltd.
Pearson Educación de Mexico, S.A. de C.V.
Pearson Education—Japan
Pearson Education Malaysia, Pte. Ltd.

Library of Congress Cataloging-in-Publication Data

Huntsman, Jon M.
  Winners never cheat : even in difficult times / Jon M. Huntsman.
     p. cm.
  Rev. ed. of: Winners never cheat : everyday values that we learned as children (but may have forgotten). 2005.
  ISBN 0-13-700903-8 (hbk. : alk. paper) 1. Business ethics. 2. Success in business—Moral and ethical aspects. 3. Executives—Conduct of life. 4. Huntsman, Jon M. 5. Businessmen—United States—Biography. I. Title.
  HF5387.H863 2009
  174'.4—dc22
                                        2008041502

To Karen,
my partner and
best friend.

CONTENTS

ACKNOWLEDGMENTS

I wish to convey my great appreciation to Jay Shelledy, a professional writer and editor, who challenged and organized my thoughts and helped convert them to the written word, and to Pam Bailey, my dedicated and loyal administrative assistant who eased the hassle with those astounding and generally unknown complexities of writing a book.

I also desire to thank deeply the professionals at Prentice Hall: Vice President and Publisher Tim Moore, and Associate Publisher and Director of Marketing Amy Neidlinger, for their initial faith and encouragement that I publish an updated version; and Operations Manager Gina Kanouse for her valuable suggestions on this edition. Thanks also goes to Pearson Education Senior Vice President of Sales and Marketing Logan Campbell, and Marketing Director John Pierce, for their unwavering commitment to and patience with a first-time author; Development Editor Russ Hall, for clear and candid critiques; Managing Editor Kristy Hart, and Copy Editors, Keith Cline and

Sarah Kearns, for their swift, quality-enhancing suggestions to and the preparation of my manuscript; and Wharton School administrators, faculty, and students for their longstanding support in this and other endeavors.

I would be especially remiss if I did not acknowledge the contributions of Larry King, whose gracious Introduction set the tone for what follows; of Neil Cavuto, for his kind Afterword and whose own book, *More Than Money*, provided inspiration; Glenn Beck, for his kind and humbling Foreword; and of trial lawyer extraordinaire, Wayne Reaud, for his humbling Preface. They are more than just successful professionals, highly respected by their peers; they are friends of mine.

I am indebted to my mother and other family members—living and deceased—for providing models of kindness and decency, and to my late father-in-law, David Haight, who always believed in me.

My greatest debt, however, is reserved for my spouse, Karen, our 9 children, and 58 grandchildren for providing me with 68 convincing reasons why a person ought to stay the proper course.

—J.M.H.

ABOUT THE AUTHOR

Jon M. Huntsman is chairman and founder of Huntsman Corporation. He started the firm with his brother, Blaine, in 1970. By 2000, it had become the world's largest privately held chemical company and America's biggest family-owned and operated business, with more than $12 billion in annual revenues. He took the business public in early 2005. He was a special assistant to the president in the Nixon White House, was the first American to own controlling interest of a business in the former Soviet Union, and is the chairman of the Board of Overseers for Wharton School at the University of Pennsylvania, his alma mater. Mr. Huntsman also has served on the boards of numerous major public corporations and philanthropic organizations, including the U.S. Chamber of Commerce and the American Red Cross. The Business School at Utah State University is named after him, as is the basketball arena at the University of Utah. The Huntsman businesses fund the foundation that is the primary underwriter for the prestigious Huntsman Cancer Institute in Salt Lake City, which he founded. The hospital/research facility has become a leader in the prevention, early diagnosis, genetic legacies, and humane treatment of cancer. He resides with his wife, Karen, in Salt Lake City. His oldest son, Jon Jr., is governor of Utah.

FOREWORD

There is a good chance that you've never heard of Jon Huntsman. He shuns the spotlight, doesn't like to talk about himself, and likes it even less when others talk about his good works. If you've ever used a plastic plate, bowl, dish, or Styrofoam take-out food container, you have Jon Huntsman to thank. His company was the first to develop these products, along with the first plastic egg carton, the original Big Mac container, and plastic fork and spoon. The small business he started with his brother in 1970 became the largest privately held chemical company in the world.

Jon Huntsman's true legacy, however, isn't the multi-billion dollar company he built or how he revolutionized how we live with what he created, but his unwavering honor, integrity, and generosity in every aspect of his professional and personal life. In an era of high-priced lawyers and accountants always looking for the latest legal loophole or tactical advantage, Jon Huntsman has done business on a handshake. Deals valued in the hundreds-of-millions of dollars were negotiated and concluded, literally, with nothing more than both parties looking each other in the eye and shaking hands. That is Jon Huntsman's reputation and legacy.

To many people, this will be nothing more than a quaint anecdote or a nostalgic reminder of how life used to be. They argue that Jon Huntsman is a man made for a different and simpler time. I would argue that we are a people out of place. Jon is currently living the life that all of us want to live, but somehow too many people have convinced themselves that business and relationships just aren't conducted this way anymore.

They couldn't be more wrong!

I first met Jon Huntsman on a visit to Utah when a mutual friend arranged for us to have lunch together. I really didn't know a lot about Jon Huntsman, but I knew he was a self-made man and a multi-billionaire. How could I turn down lunch with a multi-billionaire? When I was told we would be having lunch at a hospital cafeteria, I thought it wasn't exactly the lifestyle of the rich and famous, but I soon came to realize that the cafeteria at the Huntsman Cancer Institute is not your typical cafeteria.

Some of the best prime rib I have ever eaten was during that lunch. How could hospital food taste so good? I learned that prior to the opening of the Huntsman Cancer Institute, Jon Huntsman battled cancer. During his hospitalization and course of treatment, Jon and other cancer patients would be hungry at 3 o'clock in the morning or 9 o'clock at night, but the kitchen was closed, and when it was open, the food was bland. So when Jon opened up his cancer center, he decided to have "five-star" dining for everybody. The patients can order whatever they want, whenever they want it, because Jon doesn't want them or their families worrying about being hungry or eating bland food while fighting cancer. They have other things to focus on.

The Huntsman Cancer Institute is a marvelous and beautiful facility. As we walked through the buildings, I learned that its entire design is geared toward providing comfort, warmth, and compassion to the patients. The medical team and technology are unrivaled and unsurpassed. Halfway through our walk, Jon stopped and looked me in the eyes and said, "We're going to cure cancer here and then I'm turning this into a Ritz Carlton." I laughed and he replied, "I'm serious. We're going to cure cancer here." I believe him.

I met several grateful patients and their families. Their feelings and praise for the Huntsman Cancer Institute were universal. One patient explained how his son had been diagnosed with an aggressive form of cancer and was scheduled to fly from Philadelphia to the Huntsman Cancer Institute for an initial evaluation and treatment. They arrived at the Philadelphia Airport only to be told that all flights to Salt Lake City were cancelled due to a heavy snow storm. As this father relayed his story to me, he broke down in tears. He told me that every delay in obtaining treatment resulted in the spread of cancer in his son's body. He telephoned the Huntsman Cancer Institute and advised them of the delay and his ongoing attempts to reschedule the flight. The father was told to continue with those efforts and that the medical team would get back to him. After a few moments, a heartbroken father received a call from the Huntsman Cancer Institute. He was told that Mr. Huntsman was sending his private jet to Philadelphia to pick up both him and his son to fly them directly to Salt Lake

City. If Jon Huntsman had his way, this story would not be unique—it would be a regular occurrence.

I could spend a day sharing with you all that I learned in that short afternoon with Jon Huntsman, but it would take me a year to share with you all the things that I would like to learn from him. The way Jon conducts his business and lives his life will not only inspire you to be a better person, citizen, and entrepreneur, it also will give you hope that the good guys don't finish last.

As you read this book, I know you will feel as I did when I first read it. I hope you'll also feel compelled to share it with as many people as you can. I have never in my life purchased any book by the case, except for this one. As I meet people who question if business can be done with honesty and integrity, I send them a copy of this book to remind them that the answer is "yes," not only can it be done, it is being done.

This isn't a book limited to doing business. This isn't a book about a company that introduced the world to plastic egg cartons, plastic plates, or plastic knives and forks—this is a book about the man behind it. This is a book about life, about principles, and how success is a by-product of living those principles. This is a book about how success and blessings will rush to you by doing good first. Just ask Jon Huntsman if you'll be able to give away the money and blessings of success quickly enough.

In today's world where too many people try to grab and hoard as many dollars as they can, where politicians do anything to cling to power, where we mistakenly believe that business can no longer be done with a look in the eye and a handshake, it is time that we remember the values of honesty, integrity, and generosity. Like George Washington was in his time, Jon Huntsman is our time's "indispensable man." Look to Jon Huntsman, as he is still showing us the better way.

Glenn Beck
Glenn Beck talk show, Fox News

INTRODUCTION

GOOD TIMES, BAD TIMES

*Circumstances may change but your
values shouldn't*

When I wrote the original edition of this book in the fall of 2004, I had experienced four decades in the business world. My life had been enriched in every aspect. Like others before me, I discovered that "happiness is not the absence of conflict, but the ability to cope with it." I had witnessed it all: the greed, the cheating, the lying, and the selfishness. And the triumphs, the miracles, the rages-to-riches, and the flim-flam folks.

Or so I thought. It turned out I was wrong. There have been sequels galore on the downside (and a few on the up). As I write these lines in the fall of 2008, ethical corner-cutting has risen faster than the price of a gallon of gas. Even those tough, cold winters in rural

Idaho were easier to swallow than some of today's Wall Street trickery. Traditional values appear to be as in vogue as a subprime loan.

The good times of 2004 to 2007—record markets, sizzling real estate, easy credit, relatively acceptable energy costs—conspired to make us morally flabby. It is easy to take the high road when the route is leading to better times. Generosity isn't difficult when money flows.

Historically, positive economic scenarios are followed by painful downturns. The result presents new temptations to bend rules, to hoard material possessions, and to dismiss decency as being so last year. Born of anger, fear, stress, and frustration, the temptation to cut a corner is strong and persuasive. For the honest of heart—life's real winners—times like this are just another passing test.

When reaping an abundant harvest, most of us keep our senses—the common variety and in relation to fair play. Yet, it is quite apparent, given the amount of irresponsibility, cheating, fraudulent behavior, and pure greed that has recently been exposed, that not everyone was playing by the rules. Indeed, the breadth and depth of abhorrent behavior from this minority were startling. From subprime loan scams to speculation on the oil markets to crises in the insurance and financial sectors to falsifying the financial conditions of companies, ethical abuses, and the scope of government bailouts have been jaw-dropping.

Unfortunately, doing it the "right way" seldom cushions economic blows. Such letdowns can leave one confused and angry, but it is no time to panic, to lose track of our moral compass. On my mother's tombstone in Fillmore, Utah, are etched Shakespeare's immortal words: "Sweet are the uses of adversity." Surefire winners understand this adage. Crises must and can be resolved in moral ways. In so doing, keep in mind two things:

1. The situation hardly ever is as bad as it seems. It will pass. Better times are ahead. If nothing else, history tells us that. Americans inherently tend toward optimism. It is in our genes. The fact is, the past 20 years, overall, have been fairly good to us.

2. Prosperous times are no guarantee we will adhere to a morally righteous path. Most people strongly adhere to a fixed code of ethics whether the economy is up or down, but some feel a sense of need for even more financial gain, regardless of the consequences.

The subprime mortgage and energy price debacles were conceived in a bed of raw greed, from a dream of getting something for nothing. They were born with illusions of easy, riskless, endless money. The erosion of moral values is the natural progression of this mindset. Such obsessions require the redrawing of ethical boundaries. This sort of greed destroys the financial and emotional underpinnings of others. For some, the idea of finding a morally acceptable alternative is placed on "call waiting" until the nefarious goal is reached.

When ethical boundaries are redrawn or removed, the addiction to wealth becomes all-consuming. When expediency trumps propriety, it results in an escalating toboggan ride down a mountainside, a descent impossible to stop until the sled crashes from excessive speed and lack of direction. The late '90s dot-com burst was evidence enough. Perhaps the hedge funds of today will be the next exhibit.

This scenario results from a flawed rationale. The "objective" or "goal" is an illusion because it is based on an ethically bankrupt premise from which nothing positive can be achieved. The goal can never be reached. There will never be "enough" money; there will never be "enough" power. Thus, the "success" some envision will never be attained. A crash nearly always follows a dizzying display of "success" that is not solidly based in economic and ethical fundamentals. You can be sure the Piper will demand payment.

If everything were fair in life, perpetrators of economic meltdowns would be the only ones who suffered for their impropriety. But life isn't fair, and the fallout too often envelops good people who played by the rules, who trusted institutions, who are left to survive the rocky times brought on by others. The innocent are made to suffer for the sins of the reckless, the greedy, the cheats, the fast-buckers, the indecent, and the liars. With tough times comes another kind of temptation: the perceived necessity to cut corners, to cling to what you have, to rationalize that traditional values can be jettisoned if the ship is sinking. During this period, one can easily fall into the trap described by William Wrigley, Jr.: "A man's doubts and fears are his worst enemy."

The confusion, frustration, stress, and fears that come with financial dilemmas can make even the most ethical of individuals vulnerable to bad choices. Nevertheless, reminding ourselves of the moral path and disciplining ourselves to follow it can sustain us in such trying moments. If there is a silver lining to bad times, it is this: When facing severe challenges, your mind normally is at its sharpest. Humans seldom have created anything of lasting value unless they were tired or hurting.

❖

A discussion involving ethics can be easily misunderstood by some minds. In reality, it is quite simple. The adherence to an ethical code is best defined as how one honors a bad situation or a bad deal. Heaven knows it is easy enough to honor a good deal, or to take advantage of an event or circumstance that is rewarding and beneficial to all sides.

My company, Huntsman Corp., has completed a court trial in Delaware, as I write this. The entire case centered around the other party trying to break a contract with us. Economic conditions changed somewhat between entering the contract a year ago and when it was to be executed, and the other company's prospects of going forward are far bleaker than when they signed the deal.

One of the lawyers for the company that signed the "iron-clad" contract with us but tried to back out made an interesting statement to the judge. "This is a very tight contract," she told the judge.

"Therefore, we must look for any loopholes possible to try and extricate my client from honoring the contract." The judge didn't buy it and required the company to keep its word.

Unfortunately, this sort of behavior happens on too many occasions. With crafty lawyers, it sometimes works. Most of the time, however, iron-clad contracts simply are what they were intended to be from the start: maintaining a binding agreement between two parties. And how one honors situations when things turn sour or when a deal ends up being more costly than originally thought is how one defines his or her personal values.

In survey after survey, Americans of all stripes—Republicans, Democrats, Baptists, Jews, Unitarians, liberals, conservatives, the rich, and the poor—indicate they are worried about values. I certainly am. Some shout their angst for all to hear; others express their concerns quietly. Civilization has basic standards for proper and right-thinking action. That was the theme of *Winners Never Cheat: Everyday Values We Learned as Children (But May Have Forgotten)* when it was first published, and it remains so with this updated version.

I don't have to paint detailed landscapes. Each reader is able to point to his or her own painful experiences starting in 2007. The scenario is neither mysterious nor coincidental: Unbridled greed often prompted unethical, reckless behavior that temporarily turned on the money spigot and fueled the hysteria for many. The shock, anger, and heartbreak took place in Act II.

❖

The twin tragedy is that generosity becomes expendable in times of contraction. The basic urge to share, instilled in us from youth, is dulled by the self-centered instinct to survive. Is anyone surprised that charitable donations decreased in the second half of 2007 and have tanked in 2008? Are we surprised that civility and decency have taken back seats when we are in survival mode? Yet, tolerance and charity also are pillars of ethical behavior. In good times and in bad, our values insist we act graciously and generously.

Most of us care about one another. Human beings have considerably more in common with one another than they do differences. One's religion, political persuasion, family, financial and social status, or vocation does not hamper the common thread of personal decency running through most of humankind. In spite of America's fervent embrace of self-reliance, the vast majority of us believe in taking care of one another. Albert Schweitzer said it well: "You don't live in a world all your own. Your brothers are here, too."

An ethical code of conduct is a nondenominational religion to which all but hardcore sociopaths can subscribe. Ethical responsibility is the gold standard for determining civilized, decent courses of action. Without established and commonly accept values, the earth turns into a global food fight.

It is important for societies to settle on a set of values common to most and generally applicable to most every instance. There cannot be separate sets of ethics for home, for work, for church, and for play. Ethics belong in the home and the boardroom. And although it may seem that playing fields have changed because of unusual pressures or that rules have become malleable to accommodate unexpected situations, core values remain as solid as concrete.

❖

Because of recent events, I saw a need to write an updated version of this book—not that what I said the first time is no longer in play. On the contrary—it remains as relevant today as it did when I originally wrote it, as unchanged as when I first learned ethical principles six decades ago. It will hold true 60 decades from now, as well.

This version of *Winners Never Cheat* is presented as a warning that in the darkest of times, temptation will be most alluring. These are times for a mid-course pep talk, a reminder to stay the course, to run the good race, to fight the good fight, to follow the rules we learned long ago. They will see us through hardships and help us make ourselves and the world better off.

Periodic reviews of one's ethical stances are healthy. Times change, situations change, lives change, technology changes. Situations may be altered; basic values must not.

The simplest rules of good behavior injected into us as children, like vaccines, become the prompts for ethical behavior as adults.

Tough times must not be allowed to vanquish us. We are equipped with the values that have accompanied us since our earliest years. That preparation provides us with the strength to weather storms.

Sail on...

IF THE GAME RUNS SOMETIMES AGAINST US AT HOME, WE MUST HAVE PATIENCE TILL LUCK TURNS, AND THEN WE SHALL HAVE AN OPPORTUNITY OF WINNING BACK THE PRINCIPLES WE HAVE LOST, FOR THIS IS A GAME WHERE PRINCIPLES ARE AT STAKE.

—THOMAS JEFFERSON

COMMERCE WITHOUT MORALITY.
—THE FOURTH OF GANDHI'S SEVEN SINS

CHAPTER ONE

LESSONS FROM THE SANDBOX

*Everything we need for today's marketplace
we learned as kids.*

Growing up poor in rural Idaho, I was taught to play by the rules. Be tough, be competitive, give the game all you have—but do it fairly. They were simple values that formed a basis for how families, neighborhoods, and communities behaved. My two brothers and I had something in common with the kids on the upscale side of the tracks: a value system learned in homes, sandboxes, playgrounds, classrooms, Sunday schools, and athletic fields.

Those values did not lose their legitimacy when I became a player in the business world. Yet they are missing in segments of today's marketplace. Wall Street overdoses on greed. Corporate lawyers make fortunes by manipulating contracts and finding ways out of signed deals. Many CEOs enjoy princely lifestyles even as stakeholders lose their jobs, pensions, benefits, investments, and trust in the American way.

Cooked ledgers, irresponsibility, look-the-other-way auditors, kickbacks, and flimflams of every sort have burrowed into today's corporate climate. Many outside corporate directors bask in perks and fees, concerned only in keeping Wall Street happy and their fees intact.

In the past 20 years, investor greed has become obsessive and a force with which CEOs must deal. Public companies are pushed for higher and higher quarterly performances lest shareholders rebel. Less-than-honest financial reports are tempting when

Less-than-honest financial reports are tempting when the market penalizes flat performances and candid accounting.

the market penalizes flat performances and candid accounting. Wall Street consistently signals that it is comfortable with the lucrative lie.

Although I focus much of my advice on business-oriented activities, the world I know best, these principles are equally applicable to professionals of all stripes and at all levels, not to mention parents, students, and people of goodwill everywhere.

In the 2004 U.S. presidential election, morality issues influenced more votes than any other factor, but a Zogby International poll revealed that the single biggest moral issue in voters' minds was not abortion or same-sex marriage. Greed and materialism far and away was cited as the most urgent moral problem facing America today. (A close second was poverty/economic justice.)

In nearly a half century of engaging in some sort of business enterprise, I have seen it all. I continue to ask myself, perhaps naively so, why lying, cheating, misrepresentation, and weaseling on deals have ingrained themselves so deeply in society? Could it be that material success is now viewed to be more virtuous than how one obtains that success? One might even be tempted to believe that the near-sacred American Dream is unobtainable without resorting to moral mischief and malfeasance. To that I say, "Nonsense." Cutting ethical corners is the antithesis of the American Dream. Each dreamer is provided with an opportunity to participate on a playing field made level by honor, hard work, and integrity.

In spite of its selectivity and flaws, the American Dream remains a uniquely powerful and defining force. The allure stands strong and self-renewing, but never as feverish as in pursuit of material gain. Achieving your dream requires sweat, courage, commitment, talent, integrity, vision, faith, and a few breaks.

The ability to start a business from scratch, the opportunity to lead that company to greatness, the entrepreneurial freedom to bet the farm on a roll of the marketplace dice, the chance to rise from clerk to CEO are the feedstock of America's economic greatness.

The dot-com boom of the 1990s, although ultimately falling victim to hyperventilation, is proof that classrooms, garages, and basement workshops, crammed with doodlings and daydreams, are the petri dishes of the entrepreneurial dream. In many ways, it has never been easier to make money—or to ignore traditional moral values in doing so.

In many ways, it has never been easier to make money—or to ignore traditional moral values in doing so.

Throughout this nation's history, a spontaneous and unfettered marketplace has produced thundering examples of virtue and vice—not surprising in that very human heroes and villains populate the business landscape. Yet, a new void in values has produced a level of deception, betrayal, and indecency so brazen as to be breathtaking.

Many of today's executives and employees—I would like to think the majority—are not engaged in improper behavior. Most of the people I have dealt with in four decades of globetrotting are men and women of integrity and decency, dedicated individuals who look askance at the shady conduct of the minority.

I have known enough business executives, though, who, through greed, arrogance, an unhealthy devotion to Wall Street, or a perverted interpretation of capitalism, have chosen the dark side. Their numbers seem to be growing.

The rationale that everyone fudges, or that you have to cheat to stay competitive, is a powerful lure, to be sure.

The rationale that everyone fudges, or that you have to cheat to stay competitive, is a powerful lure, to be sure. The path to perdition is enticing, slippery, and all downhill.

The path to perdition is enticing, slippery, and all downhill. Moral bankruptcy is the inevitable conclusion.

What's needed is a booster shot of commonly held moral principles from the playgrounds of our youth. We all know the drills: Be fair, don't cheat, play hard but decently, share and share alike, tell the truth, keep your word. Although these childhood prescriptions may appear to have been forgotten or lost in the fog of competition, I believe it is more a matter of values being expediently ignored. Whatever the case, it's time to get into ethical shape with a full-scale behavioral workout program.

Financial ends never justify unethical means. Success comes to those who possess skill, courage, integrity, decency, commitment, and generosity. Men and women who maintain their universally shared values tend to achieve their goals, know happiness in home and work, and find greater purpose in their lives than simply accumulating wealth. Nice guys really can—and do—finish first in life.

Nice guys really can and do finish first in life.

❖

I worked as White House staff secretary and a special assistant to the president during the first term of the Nixon administration. I was the funnel through which passed documents going to and from the president's desk. I also was part of H. R. Haldeman's "super staff." As a member of that team, Haldeman expected me to be unquestioning. It annoyed him that I was not. He proffered blind loyalty to Nixon and demanded the same from his staff. I saw how power was abused, and I didn't buy in. One never *has* to.

I was asked by Haldeman on one occasion to do something "to help" the president. We were there to serve the president, after all. It seems a certain self-righteous congresswoman was questioning one of Nixon's nominations to head an agency. There were reports that the nominee had employed undocumented workers in her California business.

Haldeman asked me to check out a factory previously owned by this congressman to see whether the report was true. The facility happened to be located close to my own manufacturing plant in Fullerton, California. Haldeman wanted me to place some of our Latino employees on an undercover operation at the plant in question. If there had been employment of undocumented immigrants, the information would be used, of course, to embarrass the political adversary.

An amoral atmosphere had penetrated the White House. Meetings with Haldeman were little more than desperate attempts by underlings to be noticed. We were all under the gun to produce solutions. Too many were willing to do just about anything for Haldeman's nod of approval. That was the pressure that had me picking up the phone to call my plant manager.

There are times when we react too quickly to catch the rightness and wrongness of something immediately. We don't think it through. This was one of those times. It took about 15 minutes for my inner moral compass to make itself noticed and to swing me to the point that I recognized this wasn't the right thing to do. Values that had accompanied me since childhood kicked in.

Halfway through my conversation, I paused. "Wait a minute, Jim," I said deliberately to the general manager of Huntsman Container, "Let's not do this. I don't want to play this game. Forget I called."

I instinctively knew it was wrong, but it took a few minutes for the notion to percolate. I informed

Haldeman that I would not have my employees spy or do anything like it. To the second most powerful man in America, I was saying no. He didn't appreciate responses like that. He viewed them as signs of disloyalty. I might as well have been saying farewell.

So be it, and I did leave within six months of that incident. My streaks of independence, it turned out, were an exercise in good judgment. I was about the only West Wing staff member not eventually hauled before the congressional Watergate committee or a grand jury.

❖

Gray is not a substitute for black and white. You don't bump into people without saying you're sorry. When you shake hands, it's supposed to mean something. If someone is in trouble, you reach out.

Values aren't to be conveniently molded to fit particular situations. They are indelibly etched in our very beings as natural impulses that never go stale or find themselves out of style.

Some will scoff that this view is an oversimplification in a complex, competitive world. It indeed is simple, but that's the point! It's little more than what we learned as kids, what we accepted as correct behavior before today's pressures tempted us to jettison those values in favor of getting ahead or enhancing personal or corporate financial bottom lines.

Although the values of our youth, at least to some degree, usually are faith-based, they also are encompassed in natural law. Nearly everyone on the planet, for instance, shares the concept of basic human goodness.

Human beings inherently prize honesty over deceit, even in the remotest corners of the globe. In the extreme northeast of India, for example, there lies the semi-primitive state of Arunachal Pradesh. Few of us even know it exists. Indeed, this area is nearly forgotten by New Delhi. More than 100 tribes have their own cultures, languages, and animistic religions. Yet, they share several characteristics, including making honesty an absolute value.

How ironic, not to mention shameful, that the most educated and industrialized nations seem to have the most troublesome time with universal values of integrity, while semi-primitive groups do not.

Michael Josephson, who heads the Josephson Institute of Ethics in Marina del Rey, California, says one only has to view popular shows such as *The Apprentice* and *Survivor* to get the notion that life's winners are those who deceive others without getting caught. Nobody seems offended by that. It's not so much that temptations are any greater today, Josephson notes, it's that our defenses have weakened.

Be that as it may, I maintain that each of us knows when basic moral rules are bent or broken. We even are aware when we are approaching an ethical boundary. Whatever the expedient rationale or instant gratification that "justified" stepping over that line, we don't feel quite right about it because we were taught better.

It is this traditional set of behavioral values that will lead us not into temptation but to long-term success. Forget about who finishes first and who finishes last. Decent, honorable people finish races—and their lives—in grand style and with respect.

The 20th-century explorer Ernest Shackleton, whose legendary, heroic exploits in Antarctica

Forget about who finishes first and who finishes last. Decent, honorable people finish races—and their lives—in grand style and with respect.

inspired half a dozen books, looked at life as a game to be played fairly and with honor:

> *Life to me is the greatest of all games. The danger lies in treating it as a trivial game, a game to be taken lightly, and a game in which the rules don't matter much. The rules matter a great deal. The game has to be played fairly or it is no game at all. And even to win the game is not the chief end. The chief end is to win it honorably and splendidly.*

❖

The principles we learned as children were simple and fair. They remain simple and fair. With moral compasses programmed in the sandboxes of long ago, we can navigate career courses with values that guarantee successful lives, a path that is good for one's mental and moral well-being, not to mention long-term material success, if we but check those compasses on a regular basis.

WHEN YOUNG MEN OR WOMEN ARE
BEGINNING LIFE, THE MOST IMPORTANT
PERIOD, IT IS OFTEN SAID, IS THAT IN
WHICH THEIR HABITS ARE FORMED.
THAT IS A VERY IMPORTANT PERIOD.
BUT THE PERIOD IN WHICH THE IDEALS
OF THE YOUNG ARE FORMED AND ADOPT-
ED IS MORE IMPORTANT STILL. FOR THE
IDEAL WITH WHICH YOU GO FORWARD TO
MEASURE THINGS DETERMINES THE
NATURE, SO FAR AS YOU ARE CONCERNED,
OF EVERYTHING YOU MEET.
—HENRY WARD BEECHER

IT IS NOT OUR AFFLUENCE, OR OUR
PLUMBING, OR OUR CLOGGED FREEWAYS
THAT GRIP THE IMAGINATION OF OTHERS.
RATHER, IT IS THE VALUES UPON WHICH
OUR SYSTEM IS BUILT.
—SEN. J. WILLIAM FULBRIGHT

CHAPTER TWO

CHECK YOUR MORAL COMPASS

*We know darn well what is
right and wrong.*

No one is raised in a moral vacuum. Every mentally balanced human recognizes basic right from wrong. Whether a person is brought up as Christian, Jew, Buddhist, Muslim, Hindu, Unitarian, New Age, a free thinker, or an atheist, he or she is taught from toddler on that you shouldn't lie, steal, cheat, or be deliberately rude, and that there are consequences for doing so.

There is no such thing as a moral agnostic. An amoral person is a moral person who temporarily—and often quite creatively—disconnects from his or her values. Each of us possesses a moral GPS, a compass or conscience, if you will, programmed by parents, teachers, coaches, clergy, grandparents,

There is no such thing as a moral agnostic. An amoral person is a moral person who temporarily and creatively disconnects his actions from his values.

uncles and aunts, scoutmasters, friends, and peers. It came with the package, and it continues to differentiate between proper and improper courses until the day we expire.

When I was 10 years old, there resided several blocks from our home Edwards Market, one of those old houses with the grocery store in the front and the proprietors' residence in the back. It was only 200 or 300 square feet in size, but at my age the place looked like a supermarket. At the time, I was making about 50 cents a day selling and delivering the local newspaper.

I entered the store while on my route one day, and no one seemed to be around. Ice cream sandwiches had just come on the market. It was hot, and I wanted to try one. I reached inside the small freezer and grabbed an ice cream bar. I slipped the wrapped sandwich into my pocket. Moments later, Mrs. Edwards appeared, asking if she could help me.

"No, thanks," I answered politely and headed for the door. Just before it slammed shut, I heard her say, "Jon, are you going to pay for that ice cream sandwich?" Embarrassed, I turned around and sheepishly walked back to the freezer where my slightly shaking hand returned the ice cream sandwich to its rightful place. Mrs. Edwards never said another word.

It was a necessary lesson for a young, adventuresome boy, one that I have not forgotten 60 years later. It wasn't at the moment of being exposed that I suddenly realized I had done something wrong. I knew it the second I slipped my hand into the freezer, just as I would know today if I pulled a similar, but more sophisticated, stunt in a business transaction. Each of us is taught it is wrong to take that which doesn't belong to us.

Certain types of behavior encourage a disconnect with our inner compass or conscience: Rationalizing dims caution lights, arrogance blurs boundaries, desperation overrides good sense. Whatever the blinders may be, the right-wrong indicator light continues to flash all the same. We might not ask, but the compass tells.

Whatever the blinders may be, the right-wrong indicator light continues to flash all the same. We might not ask, but the compass tells.

Some point out that today's society tolerates too much questionable activity, making it difficult for the younger generation to get a consistent fix on right and wrong. Little wonder, goes this line of thought, that when the newest batch of apprentices bolt from their classrooms, their values are open to negotiation.

I am aware of polls showing that the older generation views the younger generations as less grounded in ethics, but I am not totally buying that line of thought. Society certainly is more permissive than when I was a child, but does anyone today truly condone stealing? Some modern teens may dismiss it, but does any student not consider cheating intrinsically wrong, no matter how many of their friends do it? Does society accept cooking corporate books, embezzlement, fraud, or outlandish perks for corporate executives? The answers, of course, are no.

Basic misbehavior is considered as wrong today as it was 100 years ago, although I grant that today's atmosphere produces more creative and sophisticated rationalizations for such mischief. This is why heeding the advice of George Washington, a man renowned for his integrity, is worthwhile: "Labor to keep alive in your breast that little spark of celestial fire called conscience."

Humans are the only earthly species that experience guilt. We never see our pet dogs, cats, or canaries acting chagrined for eating too much food or forgetting their manners. (And heaven knows some of them abuse the system.) Humans are unique for their ability to recognize righteous paths from indecent ones. And when we choose the wrong route, we squirm—at least inwardly.

The needle of individual compasses points true. Conceptually, ethical routes are self-evident to reasonable persons.

❖

We are not always required by law to do what is right and proper. Decency and generosity, for instance, carry no legal mandate. Pure ethics are optional.

We are not always required by law to do what is right and proper. Decency and generosity, for instance, carry no legal mandate. Pure ethics are optional.

Laws define courses to which we *must* legally adhere or avoid. Ethics are standards of conduct that we *ought* to follow. There is some overlap of the two, but virtuous behavior usually is left to individual discretion. All the professional training in the world does not guarantee moral leadership. Unlike laws, virtue cannot be politically mandated, let alone enforced by bureaucrats, but that doesn't stop them from trying. Congress considered the corporate world today so challenged when it comes to ethics that it enacted the Sarbanes-Oxley Act in an attempt to regain credibility for the marketplace. Ultimately, though, respect, civility, and integrity will return only upon the individual-by-individual return of values.

Ethical behavior is to business competition what sportsmanship is to athletic contests. We were taught to play by the rules, to be fair, *and* to show sportsmanship. The rulebook didn't always state specifically that shortcuts were prohibited. It went without saying that every competitor ran around the oval track and didn't cut across the infield.

My grandsons have a special club called The Great, Great Guys Club (The G^3 Club). Members have to be at least six years old to attend meetings. It is not permissible to fall asleep, wet your pants, or crawl under the table, among other prohibitions. They set their own rules. Amazingly, the club is quite orderly. Because parents aren't present, it is interesting to observe the standards they establish by themselves. Here are a couple of examples (with Grandpa's literary padding):

- Do what you're supposed to when you are told to do it.
- Kindness and honesty determine heart and character.
- Never tell lies.
- Cover your mouth when you cough or sneeze.

Kids usually know proper behavior, even if they don't always show it. Their moral compasses, although still developing, are in working order. They are too young to know they can trade in their conscience for a higher credit rating at Moody's. They instinctively know a conscience at ease is a best friend. They have never heard of Sophocles, but they understand his message: "There is no witness so terrible or no accuser so powerful as the conscience."

Ever notice how little guile youngsters exhibit? How honest they are with observations? How well they play with others? How smoothly they compete when adults aren't present? Sure, there always were—and still are—periodic squabbles, teasing, and selfishness, but kids generally work it out without a 300-page rulebook or a court of law. Sandlot games are played without referees or umpires, clocks, or defined boundary lines. Vague though those lines may be, sides come to an agreement when someone stepped out-of-bounds. When kids occasionally are thoughtless, it is more a case of spontaneous reaction rather than calculated meanness.

As a rule, playground protocol requires we offer a hand up to flattened opponents, share toys, call out liars and cheaters, play games fairly, and utter expressions of gratitude and praise—*please*, *thanks*, *nice shot*, *cool*—without prompt. To paraphrase Socrates, clear consciences prompt harmony.

At times, certain students in my tenth-grade biology class would write answers to a forthcoming quiz on the palms of their hands or cuffs of their shirts. Not many tried this because everyone knew cheating was wrong. In addition to the fear of being caught, most students also longed for respect as much as good grades. Once someone saw you cheating, you were never elected to student offices or respected on the sports field. Maybe that was simply part of the innocence of the 1950s, but 21st century students still know cheating is wrong, even though they may show more indifference toward this transgression than past generations.

People often offer as an excuse for lying, cheating, and fraud that they were pressured into it by high expectations or that "everyone does it." Some will claim that it is the only way they can keep up. Those excuses sound better than the real reasons they choose the improper course: arrogance, power trips, greed, and lack of backbone, all of which are equal-opportunity afflictions. One's economic status, sphere of influence, religious upbringing, or political persuasions never seem to be factors in determining whom these viruses will next ensnare.

There is contained in every rationale and every excuse, bogus as each ultimately ends up being, an awareness of impropriety. Succeeding or getting to the top *at all costs* by definition is an immoral goal. The ingredients for long-term success—courage, vision, follow-through, risk, opportunity, sweat, sacrifice, skill, discipline, honesty, graciousness, generosity—never vary. And we all know this.

However, in the winner-take-all atmosphere of today's marketplace, shortcuts to success, at least initially, are alluring, and lying often can be lucrative. That said, scammers, cheaters, performance-enhancing drug users, shell-and-pea artists, and the like historically have never prevailed for long. And when their fall does come, it is fast, painful, embarrassing, and lasting.

> *Succeeding or getting to the top at all costs by definition is an immoral goal.*

Whether exaggerating resumés or revenues, plagiarizing or profiteering, philandering or fibbing, people nearly always attempt to justify their unethical conduct when the transgression is discovered.

Enron officials rationalized from the beginning, and the same with Tyco brass, but the improper path is never a requisite for success.

Values provide us with ethical water wings whose deployment is as critical in today's wave-tossed corporate boardrooms as they were in yesterday's classrooms.

BECAUSE JUST AS GOOD MORALS, IF THEY ARE TO BE MAINTAINED, HAVE NEED OF THE LAWS, SO THE LAWS, IF THEY ARE TO BE OBSERVED, HAVE NEED OF GOOD MORALS.
—MACHIAVELLI

THE SECRET OF LIFE IS HONESTY AND FAIR DEALING. IF YOU CAN FAKE THAT, YOU'VE GOT IT MADE.
—GROUCHO MARX

AMERICANISM MEANS THE VIRTUES OF COURAGE, HONOR, JUSTICE, TRUTH, SINCERITY, AND HARDIHOOD—THE VIRTUES THAT MADE AMERICA. THE THINGS THAT WILL DESTROY AMERICA ARE PROSPERITY-AT-ANY-PRICE... THE LOVE OF SOFT LIVING AND THE GET-RICH-QUICK THEORY OF LIFE.
—THEODORE ROOSEVELT

CHAPTER THREE

PLAY BY THE RULES

Compete fiercely and fairly—
but no cutting in line.

Which rules we honor and which we ignore determine personal character, and it is character that determines how closely we will allow our value system to affect our lives.

Early on, infused with moral purpose by those who influenced us, we learned what counted and what did not. The Golden Rule, proper table manners, respecting others, good sportsmanship, telling the truth, not to mention those often-verbalized codes of schools, clubs, and churches—no cutting in line, eat everything on your plate, respect, helping those in need, and sharing—became the foundation of our character.

Character is most determined by integrity and courage. Your reputation is how others perceive you. Character is how you act when no one is watching.

These traits, or lack thereof, are the foundation of life's moral decisions. Once dishonesty is introduced, distrust becomes the hallmark of future dealings or associations. The eighteenth-century Scottish philosopher Francis Hutcheson had this figured out: "Without staunch adherence to truth-telling, all confidence in communication would be lost."

The negotiations, however, must be fair and honest. That way, you never have to remember what you said the previous day.

Businesspeople do not place their integrity in jeopardy by driving hard bargains, negotiating intensely, or fiercely seeking every legitimate advantage. The negotiations, however, must be fair and honest. That way, you never have to remember what you said the previous day.

I bargain simply as a matter of principle, whether it is a $1 purchase or a $1 billion acquisition.

Negotiating excites me, but gaining an edge must never come at the expense of misrepresentation or bribery. In addition to being morally wrong, this version of cheating takes the fun out of cutting a deal.

Bribes and scams may produce temporary advantages, but the practice carries an enormous price tag. It cheapens the way business is done, temporarily enriches a few corrupt individuals, and makes a mockery of the rules of play.

In the 1980s, Huntsman Chemical opened a plant in Thailand. Mitsubishi was a partner in this joint venture, which we called HMT. With about $30 million invested, HMT announced the construction of a second site. I had a working relationship with the country's minister of finance, who never missed an opportunity to suggest it could be closer.

I went to his home for dinner one evening where he showed me 19 new Cadillacs parked in his garage, which he described as "gifts" from foreign companies. I explained the Huntsman company didn't engage in that sort of thing, a fact he smilingly acknowledged.

Several months later, I received a call from the Mitsubishi executive in Tokyo responsible for

Thailand operations. He stated HMT had to pay various government officials kickbacks annually to do business and that our share of this joint obligation was $250,000 for that year.

I said we had no intention of paying even five cents toward what was nothing more than extortion. He told me every company in Thailand paid these "fees" in order to be guaranteed access to the industrial sites. As it turned out and without our knowledge, Mitsubishi had been paying our share up to this point as the cost of doing business, but had decided it was time Huntsman Chemical carried its own baggage.

The next day, I informed Mitsubishi we were selling our interest. After failing to talk me out of it, Mitsubishi paid us a discounted price for our interest in HMT. We lost about $3 million short term. Long haul, it was a blessing in disguise. When the Asian economic crisis came several years down the road, the entire industry went under.

In America and Western Europe, we proclaim high standards when it comes to things such as paying bribes, but we don't always practice what we preach. Ethical decisions can be cumbersome and unprofitable in the near term, but after our refusal to pay "fees" in Thailand became known, we never had a problem over bribes again in that part of the world. The word got out: Huntsman just says no. And so do many other companies.

Once you compromise your values by agreeing to bribes or payoffs, it is difficult ever to reestablish your reputation or credibility. Therefore, carefully choose your partners, be they individuals, companies, or nations.

I have a reputation as a tough but straightforward negotiator. I deal hard and intensely—but always from the top of the deck. Because it is perceived that I usually end up on the better side of the bargain, I actually had one CEO refuse to negotiate a merger with me. He was afraid he would be perceived in the industry as having "lost his pants" or that he sold at the wrong time for the wrong price. That said, I have never had anyone refuse to deal with me for lack of trust.

Competition is an integral part of the entrepreneurial spirit and the free market. Cheating and lying are not. If the immoral nature of cheating and lying doesn't particularly bother you, consider this: They eventually lead to failure.

Remember the old chant: "Winners never cheat; cheaters never win"? And, as kids, we would chide those whom we perceived to be not telling the truth with: *Liar, liar, pants on fire.* Those childish taunts actually hold true today. Moral shortcuts always have a way of catching up.

In the Shinto religion, there is this teaching: "If you plot and connive to deceive people, you may fool them for a while and profit thereby, but you will without fail be visited by divine punishment." I hasten to add that temporal judgment also awaits. There is always a payback for indecent behavior.

Consider this parable: On a late-night flight over the ocean, the pilot announces good news and bad news. "The bad news is we have lost radio contact, our radar doesn't work, and clouds are blocking our view of the stars. The good news is there is a strong tailwind and we are making excellent time."

❖

There are many professions in which one can find examples of hollow values, but nowhere is it more evident than on Wall Street, where the ruling ethos seems to be the more you deceive the other guy, the more money you make. It was none other than Abraham Lincoln who reminded us: "There is no more difficult place to find an honest man than on Wall Street in New York City."

I have spent four decades negotiating deals on Wall Street and have found few completely honest individuals. Those who are trustworthy and honorable are rare—but wonderful professionals. Some of my closest friends are found in this small cadre, be they in New York City or Salt Lake City. Those who choose to mislead others are not always engaging in the type of corruption that sends people to prison. It is more a matter of intellectual dishonesty and lack of personal ethics. Compensation has replaced ethics as a governing principle. Wall Street has but two objectives: How much money can I make? And how fast can I make it? The markets and traditional values don't always mix well.

There are many professions in which one can find examples of hollow values, but nowhere is it more evident than on Wall Street....

Wall Street thinks there is nothing wrong with this sort of behavior because everyone does it, but the lack of a sense of integrity also produces a lack of respect. WorldCom, Tyco, Enron, and other giant companies had leaders who failed to play fair.

Because they cheated, they lost. Accumulation of power and wealth became a driving force to these executives. They forgot the golden rule of integrity: Trust is a greater compliment than affection. With integrity comes respect.

Real winners never sneak to finish lines by clandestine or compromised routes. They do it the old-fashioned way—with talent, hard work, trust, fairness, and honesty. It's okay to negotiate tough business deals, but conduct your business with both hands on the table and sleeves rolled up.

> *It's okay to negotiate tough business deals, but do it with both hands on the table and sleeves rolled up.*

Make it a point to never misrepresent or to take unfair advantage of someone. That way, you can count on second and third deals with companies after successfully completing the first one. Have as a goal both sides feeling they achieved their respective objectives.

In 1999, I was in fierce negotiations with Charles Miller Smith, then president and CEO of Imperial Chemical Industries of Great Britain, one of that nation's largest companies. We wanted to acquire some of ICI's chemical divisions. It would be the largest deal of my life, a merger that would double the size of Huntsman Corp. It was a complicated transaction with intense pressure on each side. Charles needed to get a good price to reduce some ICI debt; I had a limited amount of capital for the acquisition.

During the extended negotiations, Charles' wife was suffering from terminal cancer. Toward the end of our negotiations, he became emotionally distracted. When his wife passed away, he was distraught, as one can imagine. We still had not completed our negotiations.

I decided the fine points of the last 20 percent of the deal would stand as they were proposed. I probably could have clawed another $200 million out of the deal, but it would have come at the expense of

Charles' emotional state. The agreement as it stood was good enough. Each side came out a winner, and I made a lifelong friend.

❖

Every family, home, and school classroom has its standards. There is little confusion over boundary lines. Even when one professes not to understand the rules when caught breaking them is an acknowledgment that a transgression has occurred. But what happens when some of these children turn into adults? Why are these home and classroom rules at times ignored? Why is improper behavior rationalized, even justified, when inside we know better? Some sinister force must take over in the late teens in which finding ways to circumvent traditional standards becomes acceptable.

As a teenager, my father would order me to be home by 8 o'clock. He didn't say "a.m." or "p.m." I knew he meant 8 that night. There was no fine print detailing what was meant when he said he did not want "me" driving the family Ford. Although technically, he only said I shouldn't drive that 1936 Ford coupe, he also was including my friends. (A lawyer might have counseled that, technically, only I was prohibited. Unless my dad specifically stipulated my buddy or class of people in that prohibition, anyone but me was legally allowed to drive. But I knew better.)

As we grow older, our rationale for cutting corners would make a master storyteller green with envy. We blame situations or others. The dog ate the homework that we ignored. We rationalize that immoral behavior is accepted practice. Shifting responsibility away from ourselves has become an art form.

In fact, we employ the same feeble excuses we did as children when we were caught doing something improper, something we knew we shouldn't be doing. Adults somehow have convinced ourselves we are more convincing. We aren't. The "everyone does it" line didn't work as a teenager, and it won't work now. It's a total copout and easily trumped. Everybody is not doing it. Even if they were, it still is wrong—and we know it's wrong.

Then there's that old, sheepish excuse: "The devil made me do it." The devil never *makes* you do anything. Be honest. Improper actions often appear to be easier routes, or require no courage, or are temporarily advantageous.

If only Richard Nixon had admitted mistakes up front and taken responsibility for the improper

The devil never makes you do anything. Be honest. Improper actions often appear to be easier routes, or require no courage, or are temporarily advantageous.

conduct of his subordinates, something deep down he knew to be wrong, the American public would have forgiven him. With a sense of contrition, he could have created a presidential bench-mark.

❖

Children observe their elders so they know how to act. Employees watch supervisors. Citizens eye political leaders. If these leaders and role models set bad examples, those following frequently follow suit. It's that simple.

There are no moral shortcuts in the game of business—or in the game of life. There are, basically, three kinds of people: the unsuccessful, the temporarily successful, and those who become and remain successful. The difference, I am convinced, is character.

PEOPLE SEE SUCCESSES THAT MEN HAVE MADE AND SOMEHOW THEY APPEAR TO BE EASY. BUT THAT IS A WORLD AWAY FROM THE FACTS. IT IS FAILURE THAT IS EASY. SUCCESS IS ALWAYS HARD. A MAN CAN FAIL EASILY; HE CAN SUCCEED ONLY BY PAYING OUT ALL THAT HE HAS AND IS.
—HENRY FORD

A SHIP IN HARBOR IS SAFE, BUT THAT IS NOT WHAT SHIPS ARE BUILT FOR.
—WILLIAM SHEDD

CHAPTER FOUR

SETTING THE EXAMPLE

*Risk, responsibility, reliability—
the three Rs of leadership.*

I have always loved the biblical passage,
"Whatsoever a man soweth, that shall he also
reap." It describes leadership responsibility clearly
and concisely, the precise spot where the buck
stops. The lesson is clear: Careful cultivation pays
off. Parents and employers who nurture, praise, and
when necessary, discipline fairly, experience happier
and more successful lives for themselves and those
in their charge.

Nothing new, you say? I agree, but we need
periodic reminders of this point to help overcome
unforeseen or uncontrollable obstacles that cloud
consciences and end results.

In the marketplace, we may do everything in our power to reap plentiful profits, but because of good-faith miscalculations, malevolence, negative markets, or acts of nature, a successful yield escapes us. My youthful years spent working on a potato farm taught me how an early frost or heavy rains can adversely affect the harvest no matter how carefully we tended the crop.

Fumbling by our own hand or someone else's also can ruin things. In spite of inspired vision, the purest of intentions, exemplary dedication, the greatest skills, and the most ethical of conduct, material success is never guaranteed. What is important is that the person in charge takes responsibility for the outcome, be it good, bad, or ugly. Surround yourself with the best people available and then accept responsibility.

As an officer aboard the *U.S.S. Calvert* in the South China Sea in 1960, I learned this lesson first-hand. My commanding officer, Captain Richard Collum, was a World War II veteran whom I greatly admired. On one occasion, we were to rendezvous the ships of our squadron with naval ships from seven other nations. The *Calvert* was carrying the admiral or, in naval parlance, the Flag. Every ship followed the lead of the flagship.

It was 4 a.m. and I was the officer of the deck. As a 23-year-old lieutenant (j.g.), I had much to learn in life, yet I alone had been given the great responsibility of directing the formation of the ships during those early morning hours.

At 4:35 a.m., I ordered the helmsman: "Come right to course *335*." The helmsman shouted back confirmation, as is traditional in the navy: "Coming right to course *355*."

I thought all was well, but I had not clearly heard his erroneous response. He thought I had ordered "355" degrees, rather than "335." As we made the incorrect turn, the remaining ships followed. We were off course by 20 degrees.

Some of the ships realized the error and returned to the proper course. Others did not. The formation was in dangerous disarray. Avoiding collisions caused a massive entanglement—and it was my fault. Fortunately, no damage was done, except to my self-confidence. I felt a sense of ruination and failure. How could one issue an order to the helmsman, have it reported back in error, and not catch the discrepancy? After all, repeating the order is the flashing red light for alerting one to such misunderstandings.

Learning of the debacle, Captain Collum came running to the bridge in his bathrobe and immediately took over, relieving an embarrassed young lieutenant. I was devastated. The 42 ships in our squadron took several hours to realign. Later, when the seas were calm and order had been restored, the captain called me to his cabin.

"Lt. Huntsman," he said, "you learned a valuable lesson today."

"No, sir," I responded, "I felt a great sense of embarrassment and I let down you and my shipmates."

"To the contrary, lieutenant, now you never again will permit such an act to occur. You will stay on top of every order you ever give. This will be a life-long learning experience for you. I am the captain of the ship. Everything that happens is my responsibility. You may not have caught the helmsman's mistake, but I am responsible for it. The Navy would hold a court martial for me if any of the ships had collided during that exercise."

I learned then and there what it means to be a leader. Even though the commanding officer was asleep, my actions were his actions. I also learned another lesson: By reassuring a young lieutenant that he still had the captain's confidence, he extended hope for the future.

I would repeat that scenario (the captain's, not the lieutenant's) many times as head of Huntsman Corp. Reprove faults in a way that keeps intact self-confidence and commitment to do better. As a CEO, I accepted responsibility for our plants, even though some of them were a half a world away. CEOs are charged by their directors to guarantee the good conduct and safety of employees and the company.

❖

The marketplace has many leaders—certainly in title. Leadership in the true sense of the word, I'm afraid, is not so abundant. The top executives of some leading businesses haven't the slightest idea of the breadth of stakeholder expectations. That's the result of "leaders" simply being appointed to the position or who find themselves at the top of a corporate chart, next in line for the top job. Real leadership demands character.

Leadership is found in all walks of society: business, political, parental, organized sports, military, religious, media, intellectual, entertainment, academic, the arts, and so forth. In every instance, leadership cannot exist in a vacuum. By definition, it requires others, those who would be led—and seldom are they a docile group. Humans, by nature, don't manage well.

> *Effective, respected leadership is maintained through mutual agreement. Leadership demanded is leadership denied.*

Effective, respected leadership is maintained through mutual agreement. Leadership demanded is leadership denied. Leadership is not meant to be dominion over others. Rather, it is the composite of characteristics that earns respect, results, and a continued following.

❖

Leadership demands decisiveness, and that is why it is absolutely critical that leaders know the facts. To ensure that critical information and solid advice reaches them, leaders must surround themselves with capable, strong, competent advisors—and then listen.

Unfortunately, many companies and organizations are led by executives who fear bold, candid, and talented subordinates. They seek only solicitous yes-types. They embrace adulation, not leadership. The great industrialist Henry J. Kaiser had no time for spineless messengers. "Bring me bad news," he demanded of subordinates. "Good news weakens me."

It also matters that top leaders have experience. In times of crisis, experience counts. Soldiers in combat situations prefer to follow battle-tested veterans rather than fuzzy-faced lieutenants fresh out of ROTC. It's no different in other walks of life.

Leaders must show affection and concern for those under their responsibility. Those who would render loyalty to a leader want to know they are appreciated. Whether or not they realize it, executives in leadership roles solely for the four Ps—pay, perks, power, and prestige—essentially are on their way out.

❖

Leadership is about taking risks. If your life is free of failure, you aren't much of a leader. Take no

Leaders are called on to enter arenas where success isn't covered by the warranty, where public failure is a real possibility.

risks, and you risk more than ever. No pain, no gain. Leaders are called on to enter arenas where success isn't covered by the warranty, where public failure is a real possibility. It's a scary scenario.

A 2004 survey found that three in five senior executives at Fortune 1,000 companies have no desire to become a CEO. That's twice the number compared to the first such survey conducted in 2001. Why? The risks.

The chance of making mistakes increases dramatically with leadership, no matter its nature or level, but never having failed is never having led.

To succeed, we must attempt new things. Success rates were never a consideration as youngsters when we tried our first hesitant steps, when we learned to use a toilet, when it came to correctly aiming the spoon at an open mouth, or when we decided it was time to tie our own shoelaces. As children, we understood fumbling comes with beginnings. Temporary failures never got in the way of those grand, early-life ventures.

Mistakes are not the problem. How one identifies and corrects errors, how one turns failure into a new opportunity, and how one learns from those mistakes, determines the quality and durability of leaders. Nixon's Watergate wasn't so much a burglary as it was the failure to recognize mistakes, to take responsibility for them, and to apologize accordingly.

Those who prefer jeering and ridiculing on the sidelines when the players err or stumble just don't get it: Mistakes and miscues often are transformed into meaningful, successful experiences. Keep in mind the old saying: "Good judgment comes from experience, and experience comes from poor judgment."

I am reminded of a great observation from President Teddy Roosevelt in which he places the participant and the belittler in perspective:

> *It is not the critic who counts; not the man who points out how the strong man stumbles, or where the doer of deeds could have done them better. The credit belongs to the man who is actually in the arena, whose face is marred by dust and sweat and blood; who strives valiantly;*

who errs, and comes short again and again, because there is no effort without error and shortcoming; but who does actually strive to do the deeds; who knows the great enthusiasms, the great devotions; who spends himself in a worthy cause, who at best knows in the end the triumph of high achievement, and who at worst, if he fails, at least fails while daring greatly, so that his place shall never be with those cold and timid souls who know neither victory nor defeat.

True leaders ought not to worry greatly about occasional mistakes, but they must vigilantly guard against those things that will make them feel ashamed.

True leaders ought not to worry greatly about occasional mistakes, but they must vigilantly guard against those things that will make them feel ashamed.

That said, though, repeating the same mistake too many times makes one a partner to the error. Strong leaders accept responsibility for problems and deal with them swiftly and fairly. If the problem is your responsibility, so is the solution.

Risk was a favorite topic around the dinner table as my children were advancing through their elementary and high school years. It prompted a couple of my sons a few years later to immediately jump into the commodities market and lose their shirts. They misinterpreted my advice (although I admit to doing the same thing in my younger years). Leaders clearly have to take measured risks.

❖

Leaders can come in different forms and flavors, but core elements rarely vary: talent, integrity, courage, vision, commitment, empathy, humility, and confidence. The greater these attributes, the stronger the leadership.

Many business executives seek only breathtaking compensation and perks. Legions of politicians desire only to remain in office and lead with their own self-interests in mind. There are religious leaders who bathe in reverential treatment. And we all are familiar with celebrities who are addicted to adoring fans. None of that is leadership. Successful leaders maintain their positions through respect earned the old-fashioned way.

On the wall of my office, there hangs a plaque on which are inscribed the words of legendary CBS newscaster Edward R. Murrow: "Difficulty is the one excuse that history never accepts."

I made sure my children understood what that meant. Life is difficult and success even more so, but anything worth doing must be challenging. Engaging in activities devoid of difficulty, lounging in risk-free zones, is life without great meaning. Children are perceptive. They learn as much from observation as from participation, so parental leaders especially need to practice what they preach.

❖

In 2001, our company was on the verge of bankruptcy. Our high-yield bonds were trading at 25 cents on the dollar. Our financial and legal teams had brought in bankruptcy specialists from Los Angeles and New York. In their united opinion, bankruptcy was inevitable.

For me, bankruptcy was not an option. It was *our* name on the front door. Family character was at stake. Virtually all of the 87 lenders we dealt with at the time believed we would crash. Cash was tight. We were in a recession. Our industry was overproducing. Profit margins were dropping. Exports shrunk. Energy costs were spiraling out of control.

In the middle of that perfect storm, we were hit by a rogue wave, the 9/11 catastrophe.

I reminded myself in the midst of this turmoil how grateful I was that I had been chosen to lead the company at this time because I was convinced I could guide our company through this unprecedented siege. This company would not be seized by corporate lawyers, bankers, and highly paid consultants with all the answers. Not on my watch. Not one of them could truly comprehend my notions of character and integrity.

We initiated cost-cutting programs on all levels and at all geographic locations, negotiated an equity position for bondholders, and refinanced our debt with those 87 lenders. We raised additional capital to help pay down that debt. Piece by piece, we put the complex financial mosaic back together. It would have been much easier to have chosen bankruptcy, but two and a half years later, Huntsman Corp. emerged stronger than ever. Wall Street was amazed.

A crisis allows us the opportunity to dip deep into the reservoirs of our very being, to rise to levels of confidence, strength, and resolve that otherwise we didn't think we possessed.

A crisis creates the opportunity to dip deep into the reservoirs of our very being, to rise to levels of confidence, strength, and resolve that otherwise we didn't think we possessed. Through adversity, we come face to face with who we really are and what really counts.

❖

There is a great "can do" spirit in each of us, ready to be set free. We all have reserves to tap in times of danger. In a crisis, a person's mind can be brilliant and highly creative. In a crisis, true character is revealed.

Leaders are selected to take the extra steps, to display moral courage, to reach above and beyond, *and* to make it to the end zone. For, at the end of the day, leaders have to score or it doesn't count.

❖

In today's what's-in-it-for-me environment, humility is vital for good leadership. One must be teachable and recognize the value of others in bringing about positive solutions.

A few years ago, I met with my old friend Jeroen van der Veer, chief executive of Royal Dutch/Shell Group, at his office at The Hague. Jeroen was president of Shell Chemical Company in Houston during the early 1990s. It was clear to me then that he was on his way upward to the most senior position in the world's largest company. We became trusted friends.

I asked him his thoughts on leadership. "The one common value that most leaders lack today, whether in business, politics, or religion," he replied, "is humility." He cited several cases where high-profile individuals fell from exalted positions because they refused to be teachable and humble.

"They knew all the answers and refused to listen to wise and prudent counsel of others. Their prime focus should be to create other leaders, a vision for the long term and a certain modesty about their own capabilities."

Additionally, leaders need to be candid with those they purport to lead. Sharing good news is easy. When it comes to the more troublesome negative news, be candid and take responsibility. Don't withhold unpleasant possibilities; don't pass off bad news to subordinates to deliver. Level with employees about problems in a timely fashion.

When I was in the ninth grade, I secured a job assembling wagons and tricycles at a Payless Drugstore. On Christmas Eve, the store manager presented me with a box of cherry chocolates—and laid me off. I was stunned. The manager never indicated the position was temporary. It left such an awful impression on me that I vowed I would always be upfront with employees when it came to the possibility of layoffs.

❖

Leadership must be genuine, energetic, and engaged. I have served as a director on five major New York Stock Exchange boards in the past 25 years. During that time, I have met few men and women who I felt were really providing help to the companies involved. Too many times, directors regularly make foolish, Wall Street-driven decisions, harmful to the long-term health of the company, because of today's addiction to short-term gains.

You would think that most corporate directors know better. After all, they are supposed to be bright, successful individuals. Unfortunately, many of today's boards are little more than social clubs that do a poor job of protecting the long-term interests of stockholders.

Unfortunately, many of today's boards are little more than social clubs that do a poor job of protecting the long-term interests of stockholders.

Most corporate directors lack expertise in the industry of the company they are directing. Management easily manipulates such directors because the latter's chief concerns are fees, retirement benefits, and the prestige of being on a corporate board. Typically, they have only a small portion of their net worth invested in the company. They loathe being at odds with the CEO, chairman, or other directors.

Stockholders would be outraged if they knew the lack of focus, expertise, connectivity, and good judgment exhibited by a sizable number of corporate directors. Although these directors occasionally fire the CEO in a huff when a deal doesn't work out or an ethical gaffe is exposed, they would better meet their obligations if they stopped CEOs from making bad deals or unethical decisions in the first place.

Always cheer for the individual director who breaks ranks to propose a novel route, who offers a different perspective, who raises ethical concerns, or who focuses on the long-term well-being of stockholders.

I have great respect for many CEOs in today's business world. They are dedicated, gifted, and honest men and women. They appreciate why they were chosen to lead their respective companies. They accept their duties: keep business healthy; deliver a fair profit in the most professional, socially responsible way possible; display moral backbone; and are forthcoming.

❖

When the ship finds itself in trouble, as my earlier story related, all eyes turn to the captain. Subordinates may have been the ones who erred, but it is the captain who must take responsibility for the mistake and for steering the ship out of trouble. And, be assured, it takes more effort correcting a mistake than to make it.

Leadership is a privilege. Those who receive the mantle must also know they can expect an accounting of their stewardships.

It is not uncommon for people to forego higher salaries to join an organization with strong, ethical leadership. Most individuals desire leadership they can admire and respect. They want to be in sync with that brand of leader, and will often parallel their own lives after that person, whether in a corporate, religious, political, parental, teaching, or other setting.

A good example of this is Mitt Romney, former governor of Massachusetts, who returned integrity to the scandal-ridden 2002 Winter Olympics. That classic show of leadership was infectious all the way through the Olympic organization to the thousands of volunteers. As a result, those Games came off as the most successful and problem-free in recent Olympics history.

Conversely, because leaders are watched and emulated, their engagement in unethical or illegal conduct can have a devastating effect on others.

❖

Courage may be the single most important factor in identifying leadership. Individuals may know well what is right and what is wrong but fail to act decisively because they lack the courage their values require.

Leaders—whether inside families, corporations, organizations, or politics—must be prepared to stand against the crowd when their moral values are challenged. They must ignore criticism and taunts if pursuing a right and just route. Leadership is supposed to be daunting. Courage is an absolute requisite. Without it, noted Winston Churchill, other virtues lose their meaning. "Courage is the first of the human qualities because it is a quality which guarantees all the others."

Some economists argue that business leaders have but a single responsibility: to employ every *legal* means to increase corporate profits. Commercial enterprise, such economists reason, is amoral by nature. Compete openly and freely in any way you wish so long as you do not engage in deception and fraud (rule-book violations).

Embracing a credo of that nature, without proper emphasis on morality, is an invitation for executives to rationalize ethical corner-cutting and a potential blueprint for impressionable business-school students when they are turned loose on the marketplace. Humility, decency, and social leadership become irrelevant under that sort of a scenario.

The gospel according to these economists implies that if somehow one finds a loophole in a law prohibiting shortcuts across the infield, one does not have to remain on the same oval track with the other racers. One is allowed—no, obligated—to maximize results under the broadest interpretation of the official rules of conduct, however bent, loopholed, or indecent it may be.

I don't totally blame the moral briar patch in which we seem to find ourselves on that line of thought. In fact, I agree with these economists to this extent: Business itself can't have ethics any more than a building can have ethics; only humans can possess ethical standards. Where I differ is the implication that professional morals distract business executives from their fiduciary obligations.

In a technical sense, business itself may well be amoral, but its leadership must be dictated by moral decisions. It takes great courage to follow the moral compass in the face of marketplace pressures, but no challenge alters this fact: Regardless of who is holding the compass, or how they are holding it, or what time of day it happens to be, north is always north, and south is always south.

Following one's moral compass is for neither the faint of heart nor the cold of feet.

Following one's moral compass is for neither the faint of heart nor the cold of feet. Leaders worthy of the name understand and accept that they are chosen every bit as much for their values and courage as for their administrative skills, marketing savvy, and visionary outlook.

LET YOUR "YES" BE "YES" AND YOUR
"NO" BE "NO."
—JAMES 5:12

THE FIRST AMENDMENT IS 45 WORDS;
THE LORD'S PRAYER IS 66 WORDS; THE
GETTYSBURG ADDRESS IS 286 WORDS.
THERE ARE 1,322 WORDS IN THE
DECLARATION OF INDEPENDENCE,
BUT THE GOVERNMENT REGULATIONS
ON THE SALE OF CABBAGE
TOTAL 26,911 WORDS.
—NATIONAL REVIEW

ONE MAN WITH COURAGE
MAKES A MAJORITY.
—ANDREW JACKSON

CHAPTER FIVE

KEEP YOUR WORD

It's high time to corral the corporate lawyers.

Shakespeare didn't literally mean it when he said that the first thing we must do is kill all the lawyers, but you can forgive folks for smiling at the thought, given that the legal profession, collectively and with our complicity, is stripping America of personal accountability and trust. All of us, in ways large and small, partially are responsible for this erosion of integrity, but I place the greatest culpability, with notable exceptions, on attorneys—especially corporate lawyers.

Lawyers don't start out their lives wanting to do that, but they are trained in law school to gain the edge, to win rather than mediate. Under the guise of legal protection, many corporate lawyers have made it impossible to seal business deals with just a handshake. They—I trust unwittingly—have created a tidal wave of distrust, ended long-term friendships, and bartered the inherent goodwill between people for loopholes, escape clauses, and weasel wording.

One's word being one's bond has been replaced with one's word being subject to legal review.

One's word being one's bond has been replaced with one's word being subject to legal review.

Concise, straightforward transactions carry no weight unless accompanied by 100 pages of exceptions and wherebys in fine-print legalese. A deal sealed with a handshake is meaningless without a signed legal document whose complexity rivals that of the Treaty of Versailles.

This is a great weakness in our system because most lawyers have little in the way of business experience. They tend to focus on why something should not or cannot be done. Legal beagles make up the tenor and soprano sections of this choir of naysayers. Lenders, accountants, and consultants round out the hand-wringing chorale as the altos and baritones. They may hear themselves singing in perfect harmony, but to most of us it comes off as dissonance.

As Jeffrey Sonnenfeld, associate dean of executive programs at Yale School of Management, put it in a *Business Week* article, corporate attorneys are considered the "vice presidents of No."

Problems nearly always arise when clients allow lawyers to make business decisions the latter are not qualified to make. In a recent *Inc.* magazine article, author Norm Brodsky says smart lawyers understand the boundaries of their expertise and limit themselves to providing legal advice. "Not-so-smart lawyers," he says, "charge ahead and screw things up....Lawyers are not business people, although many of them would have you believe otherwise."

Many CEOs and others in the corporate hierarchy embrace every particle of "wisdom" uttered by a lawyer without realizing the person imparting the information often is the least prepared to counsel those who have developed a consistent marketplace track record.

> *Human beings are innately honest, but if you pack legal heat, the other side will do likewise.*

Human beings are innately honest, but if you pack legal heat, the other side will do likewise. At that point, it becomes negotiation by attorneys.

Lock the lawyers in the attic until you truly need them. I came to a point in my career where I tossed the lawyers out of all meetings where merger negotiations were ongoing, summoning them only when the technical expertise in law and language to make the deals was required.

It's not that lawyers are inherently unethical or evil, certainly no more so than members of any other profession. It's a matter of lawyers overriding personal ethics with professional standards. Lawyers are taught to represent the best interest of their clients even if that mandate means inflicting unnecessary harm to the other side.

Murray Swartz, a New York attorney of considerable skill and fame, who is often described as a lawyer's lawyer, maintains that when acting as an advocate for a client, a lawyer "is neither legally, professionally, nor morally accountable for the means used or the ends achieved."

Former Utah Supreme Court Chief Justice Michael Zimmerman considers such rationale as nothing more than a comfortable way to avoid ethical responsibility. Lawyers are more than amoral technicians.

Lawyers certainly are not the only professional group occasionally separating personal ethics from professional norms. Tobacco company executives, who only want to expand their markets and further their corporation's profits, cloak their consciences with the simplistic observation that no one forces people to smoke. The human toll their product extracts is not addressed in the business theories that cover the jingle of cash registers.

Politicians weasel and fib, promise much and deliver little, all in the name of remaining in public office. All's fair in love, war, the bottom line, the final score, and re-election bids.

The news media wraps itself in the mantle of the "public's right to know," shielding sloppy, unfair, or erroneous coverage with a First Amendment excuse.

And I have already expressed my opinion of Wall Street, an arena in which misinformation is considered a virtue.

My point is there are larger issues of personal ethics, integrity, and human decency that, on occasion, ought to override the traditional standards of professional practices.

I have reserved my harshest rhetoric for this problem because I feel so strongly that integrity is central to all else virtuous. It is distressing that two people these days must necessarily be uneasy about simple oral agreements or that we don't take responsibility for our own errors.

Reestablishing concepts of personal responsibility and one's word being one's bond, means kicking the lawyer dependency.

Reestablishing concepts of personal responsibility and one's word being one's bond, means kicking the lawyer dependency. We can avoid many unpleasantries, legal and social, by offering trust, accepting responsibility, and standing by our word, even when it causes discomfort.

Most spouses, neighbors, and business colleagues don't require lawyers every time there is a disagreement. If we adhere to basic moral values, voluminous legal contracts would become unnecessary.

Abraham Lincoln, himself a lawyer, was on target: "Discourage litigation. Persuade your neighbor to compromise whenever you can. As a peacemaker, the lawyer has the superior opportunity of being a good man. There will still be business enough."

There is a fun fact that suggests America has 40 lawyers for every engineer, whereas China, emerging as one of the world's most dynamic nations, has 40 engineers for every lawyer. I am not sure exactly what that says, but it can't be a plus for the United States. It may only be coincidence that the explosion in ethical and legal lapses in the business world parallels proportionately the increase in lawyers.

"Most business decisions involve risk," notes Norm Brodsky in his *Inc.* article. "That's why the business person has to make them. Who else can say how much risk he or she is willing to live with? Unfortunately, some lawyers don't understand that it's the client's responsibility…to assess risk."

Don't misunderstand. It is important that we listen to lawyers, but only for a second opinion. Your opinion ought to be the first—and the last.

> *It is important that we listen to lawyers, but only for a second opinion. Your opinion ought to be the first—and the last.*

Some of us refuse to act or to move ahead in life without legal advice. In so doing, we lose our individuality. Somebody else is thinking for us, speaking for us, acting for us, making us mistrust everyone.

The legal profession has made life far too complicated. The problem is we believe we must always have a lawyer at our side. Virtually everyone brings along a lawyer to business transactions in anticipation of the other side pulling something.

Because the devil supposedly is in the details, negotiations represent a grand and lucrative playpen for lawyers. The law, like medicine, computer programming, and lunar landings, is complicated. Most of us aren't skilled in computers, medicine, rocket science, or law. We feel we aren't in a position to question, but we are. Insist the outcome be honorable and make good business sense.

Lawyers have us trained to believe nothing is airtight, any agreement can be broken, and that life is one big loophole. A handshake ends up as meaningless as an Enron audit. Heaven forbid the law be the law. Today, the law is whatever the client

Because the devil supposedly is in the details, negotiations represent a grand and lucrative playpen for lawyers.

wants it to be. Today, we can sue anybody over anything. We can ruin a reputation with a simple allegation, trumpeting the canard worldwide on the Internet in seconds.

All that said, I have been privileged to know some wonderful lawyers who genuinely seek justice and embrace honest deals. Lawyers certainly can be helpful steering one through today's myriad government regulations and contractual prose embedded with technicalities, legal pitfalls, or unintelligible blather. And, of course, they are invaluable should you find yourself in court, more than a remote possibility in today's litigious jungle. That, though, ought to be the extent of their help.

The CEO is the individual who takes the risk; who must determine the personally decent, ethical route; who orders the speed and direction of the ship. If lawyers are allowed to decide all that, they are the ones leading the company. So far as I know, corporate attorneys are advisors.

During these litigious times, it is not surprising that more companies are seeking CEOs with legal degrees. Although there are exceptions, that seems like the wrong direction. Lawyers can be trained in accounting and finance principles, but team playing, entrepreneurial risk taking, allowing handshakes to say it all, and market vision do not readily attach themselves to those steeped in the work habits and mindsets of the legal profession.

I have observed that in most cases where the CEO is a lawyer, the company experiences a major void and, regularly, a financial catastrophe. The basic ingredients of customer satisfaction take a backseat to legalistic jargon. And heaven help suppliers and employees who want to continue a simple and straightforward relationship.

As *Business Week* noted at the end of 2004: Don't look for JD degrees to replace MBAs anytime soon.

❖

Keeping one's word often requires great resolve. Two personal examples follow.

In 1986, after lengthy negotiations with Emerson Kampen, chairman and CEO of Great Lakes Chemical Company, we agreed he would purchase 40 percent of a division of my company for $54 million. Negotiations had been long and arduous, but a handshake sealed the deal.

I didn't hear from Kampen for several months. Approximately four months after those discussions, Great Lakes lawyers called to say they would like to draft some documents. They had been dragging their feet—business as usual. It took three months for this rather simple purchase agreement to be placed on paper. The time lapse between the handshake and documents was now six and a half months.

In the interim, the price of raw materials had decreased substantially and our profit margins were reaching all-time highs. Profits had tripled in that half a year. Nothing had been signed with Great Lakes, and no documents had been exchanged. Kampen called with a remarkable proposal.

"Forty percent of Huntsman Chemical today is worth $250 million, according to my bankers," said Kampen. "You and I shook hands and agreed on a $54 million price over six months ago." Although he did not think he should have to pay the full difference, he thought it only fair he pay at least half and offered to do so.

My answer was no, it would not be fair to use the appreciated value, nor should he have to split the difference. He and I shook hands and made an agreement at $54 million, I said, and that's exactly the price at which the attorneys would draft our documents.

"But that's not fair to you," Kampen responded.

"You negotiate for your company, Emerson, and let me negotiate for mine," was my response.

Kampen never forgot that handshake. He took it with him to his grave. At his funeral, he had pre-arranged for two principal speakers: the governor of Indiana and me. I never was personally close to Emerson, but he and I both knew that a valuable lesson had been taught. Even though I could have forced Great Lakes to pay an extra $200 million for that 40 percent ownership stake in my company,

I never had to wrestle with my conscience or look over my shoulder. My word was my bond.

(It is ironic that when I wrote this revised manuscript I was involved in a business situation where the executives of the company that contractually agreed to buy my company decided they no longer wished to pay the agreed-upon price. I had to take them to court, where the judge held that the company indeed was bound by its word.)

Back in the early 1980s, my first big deal was purchasing a petrochemical facility from Shell Oil Company. Peter De Leeuw, a vice president of Shell Chemical, drew up a straightforward draft agreement. He asked me to review it overnight and the two of us would then discuss it in the morning. I read it carefully, made a few minor changes, and signed it on the spot. Although he had not as yet submitted it to the corporate attorneys, it was the shortest, best-prepared, most binding document I had ever read.

De Leeuw was taken aback by my action. He wanted my lawyers (and his) to have a look at the agreement. I said I trusted him. Although he still had Shell's attorneys look it over (they, of course, had scores of questions and additions), my immediate signing and display of trust gave De Leeuw confidence that I was serious and paved the way for his help working out one glitch after another in the months to come. When negotiating, seek out players you can trust; keep the lawyers on the bench.

I offer these episodes in no self-serving sense; it would be boorish to the reader to do so. It is imperative, though, that we all understand the importance of keeping one's word.

❖

We need not eliminate lawyers—simply reduce their modern-day omnipresence in our dealings. Use them for legal advice and leave other decisions to the experts.

Trust more in each other and in ourselves. As the late journalist and author Frank Scully once asked: "Why not go out on a limb? Isn't that where the fruit is?"

Trust, however, should not be blind. Save blind faith for religion. A prudent businessperson knows with whom he or she is negotiating and exactly what is being negotiated. When it came to this, President Ronald Reagan had a great line: "Trust but verify." If we trust in our own instincts and ability to evaluate, we will have less trouble trusting others.

As captains of our own character, it is essential we understand the great legacy of trust and

> *Trust should not be blind. Save blind faith for religion.*

integrity. We will be remembered for truthful disclosures and promises kept.

Individual and corporate integrity must become the hallmark of the marketplace. Deep in our hearts, we all have a basic understanding that when we shake on something, it's supposed to stick. Remember the "cross my heart and hope to die" line? A handshake should always be as binding as a signed legal document.

We ought to negotiate earnestly and with all diligence for the best possible outcome. When a handshake is given, it must be honored—at all costs. Tough bargaining occurs only before the deal is agreed to. When you shake hands, the negotiating is over. Your word is your greatest asset; honesty is your best virtue. Without it, Cicero believed, there is no dignity.

> *WHOEVER LOVES MONEY,*
> *NEVER HAS MONEY ENOUGH;*
> *WHOEVER LOVES WEALTH IS*
> *NEVER SATISFIED WITH HIS INCOME.*
> *—ECCLESIASTES 5:10*

CHAPTER SIX

WHY WE CROSS THE LINE
There are many temptations, but reminders help.

Why is it that some bright students choose to cheat? Why do some otherwise upstanding citizens chisel on their income tax returns? Why do some physically-fit, talented athletes inject themselves with performance-enhancing drugs? How can some folks who profess to be religious look you in the eye and tell you a lie? How is it that some law-abiding people cheat on their spouses? Why do some super-wealthy corporate executives line their already bulging wallets through fraudulent methods? And, while we are figuring out life's mysteries, why is it that some of the richest people seem to have the hardest time parting with money for those in need?

All simple questions with various and complex answers. We certainly aren't forced to perform in unethical ways, but dishonesty (and selfishness) occurs often enough, if news media, academic research, and our own experience are valid indicators. Some claim dishonesty is rampant, although there is no empirical evidence to support that contention. (Who would trust a poll of liars and cheats, in any case?) There may be less ethical behavior today, but it also is true that it is more publicized than 50 years ago. High-profile anecdotes may give the impression that it's more commonplace.

Dishonesty is not a modern phenomenon.

This I do know: Dishonesty is not a modern phenomenon.

Most of us think of ourselves as honest, decent, moral human beings—and, for the most part, we are. The apparent dilemma—our perception versus real life—suggests we are, at times, in some level of denial. In fact, we periodically engage in minor dishonest and unethical acts for a variety of reasons.

For some, the motivation may by nothing more than the cheap thrill of stepping over the line, of tempting fate. For others, the answer may lie in whether the dishonest act makes "sense" to us on a cost-benefit analysis, whether the ill-gotten gain exceeds or "justifies" the risk.

Are there times when we feel so beleaguered, we believe we have no choice but to engage in ethical corner-cutting as the only practical avenue out? Do some people experience an ethical short circuit because of the pressures? Or are they simply too self-centered to care? The reasons for improper conduct are many; the right route is but one.

Honesty is viewed by all religions and nearly every society as a virtue. Study after study reveals that people value honesty and strongly believe they are honest. We don't like to be lied to, or lose out to a

> *The reasons for improper conduct are many; the right route is but one.*

cheater, or be confronted with fraud. It angers us when public officials engage in wrongdoing and when CEOs cook private-sector books.

Furthermore, we know unethical behavior when we see it. Parents know when their children are fibbing. Recent research into a toddler's sense of values produced evidence that children as young as three years old can detect when someone is not telling them the truth.

That each of us occasionally stumbles is no revelation. Ever since Adam failed the original taste test, the world is replete with examples of individuals making bad choices. We, after all, are frail, imperfect humans, prone to mistakes. Our biases, greed, and conceit generally are the underlying causes of jumping righteous rails. The occasional slip, fortunately, does not become habitual with most of us because when we make a mistake, we feel bad, embarrassed, and guilty. Sooner or later, we own up. None of us wants to break his or her word.

Yet there are times when it is impossible to keep it. Remember, though, that a bad turn of events does not release us from our promise. Only the person to whom your word was given can release you from that. We must inform the person of our dilemma and give him or her the opportunity, if he or she so chooses, to let us off the hook.

In prosperous times, people sometimes wander from the ethical walkway, blinded by the glitter of the gold. The temptation lurks to prolong the euphoria by the easiest means possible. We may decide that engaging in ethical behavior may put us at a disadvantage with respect to how others fare. (Athletes who use performance-enhancing drugs, for example, feel that they can't afford to stop because their competitors take them.)

Unethical acts can be viewed as the more practical route. The potential penalty for dishonesty may appear small compared to the perceived advantages that it makes sense to do it.

In uncertain times, people may see dishonesty as the only way to preserve their careers, as the fastest cure to rebuilding wealth, or the only way to keep their heads above water. They may falsely believe they have nothing to lose, or that the dishonesty will only take place "just this once." It is a greasy slope, to be sure.

There is no excuse for lying, cheating, and selfishness under any circumstances, but one can see how the pressure to do so builds during a crisis. That's why I feel compelled to reissue a strong call for reaffirming our moral foundations.

Some people—probably small in number—in business, sports, academics, politics, and organizations are flat out pathologically unethical. They need help beyond what I can offer here. Additionally, there is a group of folks out there who don't give a darn about others. They are in it for themselves. This latter group is a growing problem and a menace to the values we hold dear.

We are all pulled, at times, between competing motivations: the short-term gain from cheating versus the maintenance of a positive self-image. Either choice requires a sacrifice. If the reward is not large, the cost of remaining honest is minimal. If the benefit is larger or perceived to be more necessary, the decision to remain honest becomes much harder.

This cost-benefit theory was the basis of an experiment, "The Dishonesty of Honest People," undertaken in 2005 by economists Nina Mazar and Dan Ariely of the Massachusetts Institute of Technology, and On Amir, a marketing expert at the University of California at San Diego.

Participants carefully weighed the advantages and disadvantages of honesty and dishonesty, reaching a decision that maximized their best interests, including internal rewards. The individuals were paid so much for each correct answer. In other words, if a respondent did not know the answer to a question, cheating to find the correct response would net him or her additional compensation.

Needless to say, there was considerable cheating. The threat of getting caught did not seem to figure into the equation. When the conductors of this test added a twist to the exam, however, the results were dramatic. (I will provide the details shortly.)

Winning isn't always measured in money. There will be times when one will lose money—sometimes a lot of it—but winning is much more than ledgers. In assessing our worth, look first to the bedrock of our lives: values, health, family, and friends. Dying is no fun, even if you leave behind a pot of gold. Family and friends are the lifeblood and legacy of our lives.

Our values, if properly anchored, will see us through these storms. Take a deep breath in the middle of a crisis and consider these bright stars in

Family and friends are the lifeblood and legacy of our lives.

our human solar system. If they are aligned, all is well. From there, one can set about restructuring what it is that put us in the mess. Never adjust your values downward. To do so requires that you must lie to yourself. Once you see yourself as a fraud, your positive self-image evaporates. The best way to keep that from happening when in crisis mode is to actively change the status quo. Talk to people, take a break, stuff any money left under a mattress until the hurricane blows over. Start over. (I have started over on three occasions, each time reaching or exceeding a billion dollars in value.) It can be done, and you can do it.

Now for the twist I mentioned earlier with the cheating experiment: The people in the test (and anywhere else, for that matter) knew inwardly that dishonesty is wrong. The concept of honesty was not new to them, but basic knowledge of right and wrong behavior is not always sufficient to keep people on the straight and narrow, the Mazar-Amir-Ariely study concluded. "The question is not whether a person knows it is wrong to behave dishonestly, but rather whether he or she thinks of those (moral) standards and compares his or her behavior to the standards at the moment the person is tempted to behave dishonestly."

So, in the second go-round with the 229 student participants, they were asked to complete a short assignment before taking the exam that would reward them financially for each correct answer. Half of the students were instructed to write down 10 books they had read in high school; the other half was asked to recall as many of the 10 Commandments as they could remember. There was no direct reward for either of these preliminary tasks.

On average, the participants remembered only about four of the Commandments, but it was enough. In the group that had to recall its high school reading, the cheating level was the same as the day before, but cheating was significantly lower for the group that first had to recall the Commandments, the basic moral code for a Judeo-Christian culture. In a nutshell, this is what the three researchers made of it: When reminded of our core values, the tendency for deception decreases.

When reminded of our core values, the tendency for deception decreases.

It wasn't the rules or the potential punishment that kept people honest. It was being reminded of core values embedded from our earliest days: Don't steal. Don't cheat. Don't lie.

We are in dire need of constant reminders, whether from others or from ourselves, of the universal axiom: Honesty is the best policy.

AN HONEST MAN SPEAKS THE TRUTH,
THOUGH IT MAY GIVE OFFENSE;
A VAIN MAN, IN ORDER THAT IT MAY.
—WILLIAM HAZLITT

KNOWING OTHERS IS WISDOM.
KNOWING YOURSELF IS ENLIGHTENMENT.
—LAO-TZU

CHAPTER SEVEN

PICK ADVISORS WISELY

Surround yourself with associates who have the courage to say no.

My children firmly believe I am from another age. I never learned computer skills; I don't quite understand how e-mail works. My letters and notes quite often are written by hand. I manage in today's high-tech world because there are many people around me who are technologically competent. In some ways, it leaves me in a more pleasant setting where relationships are more personable.

If you don't have knowledge of something, find people who do. I have around me wonderful men and women of talent, skill, energy, virtue, and promise. They know that Huntsman team membership requires the following:

- Adherence to proper values
- Loyalty to the company
- Loyalty to the CEO
- Competence

In sum, I look for ethical, loyal, talented associates. Finding talent is the easy part. Determining matches for the other criteria takes a skilled eye and ear. Of no consequence to me are gender, race, one's religious, political, and ethnic background, which school he or she attended, family pedigrees, hairstyles, and other such individual factors that seem to give some employers pause. Judge people by their values, character, and deeds—not by their looks, backgrounds, and philosophical beliefs.

The Huntsman employee base has been as high as 16,000, up considerably from the 200 workers when I started 35 years ago. To guide those associates, I have sought out individuals with leadership and specialty skills far beyond my own.

Life is not a game of Solitaire; people depend on one another.

Life is not a game of Solitaire; people depend on one another. When one does well, others are lifted. When one stumbles, others also are impacted.

There are no one-man teams—either by definition or natural law. Success is a cooperative effort; it's dependent upon those who stand beside you.

It has always been a source of personal strength for me to be surrounded by people who hold similar or greater values to mine, who share my passion and vision, who have capacities greater than my own.

Frequently, I am asked why Huntsman Corp. has been successful. What's the formula for starting with nothing and arriving at wealth? My initial answer is to underscore integrity, vision, commitment, generosity, self-confidence, and the courage to make decisions that set one apart from a competitor or from what currently is the marketplace norm. Then I add: The first and most important decision in one's success is carefully choosing the people who will surround you. Make sure they share your values, make certain their character defaults to high moral ground in times of stress, ensure they are bright and comprehend results, and be confident of their loyalty.

The Wall Street Journal recently ranked attributes recruiters seek in hiring new personnel. The three highest—and substantially ahead of the others—were interpersonal skills, an ability to work well within a team, and personal integrity.

Curiously, work experience and strategic thinking were in the middle of the list of the 20 most desired traits for new hires.

It does little good to employ a top sales manager, a talented computer engineer, or an outstanding production superintendent if their values don't coincide with yours. If you aren't operating under the same standards, how can associates alert you to a dangerous turn? If those associates don't know north from south or, worse, don't care, how will the organization stay on the proper course? Cultivate relationships with those who are teachable.

Backgrounds, age, education, and experience may vary with key associates, but basic values must be uniform and in compliance with the culture you want for your company, organization, or home. Constantly keep ethical expectations alive. Otherwise, brace for heavy consequences.

Like-minded associates are not always easy to locate, but the search is worth it. Together, you will be responsible for establishing and enforcing ethical standards. Together, you will set the examples. If an executive has a background of cutting corners or of dishonesty, the organization and everyone inside it eventually will pay a price.

When we were young, we unconsciously chose friends with similar values. We didn't like dealing with individuals, for example, who were not truthful. They concerned us. Lying seemed so silly, so unnecessary. Nobody likes dishonesty. I remember associating with people who often were not the most popular in the school, but they were respected. And one of the reasons they were respected was because they had integrity.

Although we regularly treat the terms as if they are equals, there is a difference between *admiration* (popularity) and *respect*. The former has to do with positive, outward attributes; the latter is a positive recognition of one's inner strength and character. We admire celebrities, but we don't necessarily respect them. We respect great teachers, but we don't always like them.

Some people earn admiration *and* respect. If you must choose one, however, go for respect every time.

Some people earn admiration and respect. If you must choose one, however, go for respect every time.

Most of us occasionally must decide between being popular and doing things that align with our personal values. Adhering to immediate gratification and expedient routes place us in danger of forfeiting the very character that produces long-term success and respect. Selecting a friend or an associate who is respected because of a devotion to values is smart. It ensures you never have to worry about that person's trustworthiness.

I once asked a group of 200 junior high and high school students the difference between respect and popularity. Their answers were interesting. One young man defined respect as "how I feel about myself when I know I am honest and have done the right thing." That was a tremendous answer because, whether he knew it or not, it is difficult for a person to respect others without having self-respect.

Asked whether an individual can enjoy respect *and* popularity, an eighth grader said that it was possible—if she sticks to her values and treats others with kindness and affection. I responded that such individuals are rare, but if a choice between the two attributes must be made, it would be well to remember that popularity is fleeting. Without lasting respect, relationships won't long survive. Stand for what is right, not what is popular.

Ethicist Michael Josephson says ethics is all about how we meet the challenge of doing the right thing when that act will cost more than we want to pay. This is precisely what I was telling those youngsters. Respect often comes at a cost—quite high at times—but one must be willing to pay the price.

❖

It is difficult within peer groups to break with the crowd, to exercise moral authority in the face of majority opposition. It takes courage to speak out when others believe that what they are doing will net them a promotion, greater popularity, additional wealth, or when that warning will jeopardize one's job or public standing. Notwithstanding those risks, remaining true to one's conscience is a powerful force.

...remaining true to one's conscience is a powerful force.

There is no book written, no guideline yet crafted, and no class lecture devised that explains how to activate courage. Courage comes from deep within one's being. Courage is not the understanding of what is right or wrong. Rather, it is the strength to choose the right course.

When we aren't focused, ethical dilemmas present themselves in the color gray. We are aware of the black and white of situations, but it is easy to conclude that we may cruise in gray areas with impunity so long as we don't drift into what is demonstrably illegal behavior. We, of course, are deluding ourselves. In these scenarios, we inevitably cross ethical boundaries somewhere prior to the behavior becoming unlawful, if we haven't already.

That's why it is critically important to choose wisely when selecting those who will be at your right and left sides, and those who have your back. They must have a keen sense of where the boundaries of life's playing field are located. Your associates must share your perception of where the out-of-bounds lines belong. Shades of gray are almost always outside the bounds of propriety. Although playing in the gray zones may not technically be illegal, it is a dangerous practice at best and an improper one at worst.

Core values, reinforced by regular consultations with one's internal compass, are more critical to a company than defined regulations. If determining

If we must check to see whether our activity is wrong, it probably is.

whether behavior is ethical automatically requires searching the official rulebook, it is an indication we are vulnerable to missing danger signs. If we must check to see whether our activity is wrong, it probably is.

❖

I have had the good fortune to be associated with people who have a marvelous "can do" attitude. They know that, at the end of the day, we can make better and more ethical decisions than the outsiders—the consultants, lawyers, and lenders. To be sure, there are bright, able, competent men and women in the fields of law, business consulting, and banking. For the most part, however, they do not take personal risks and will never know the true joy and satisfaction that comes from being in the mine-filled arenas where empires are built.

They also have a hard time seeing the responsibility and gratification of dedicating one's resources and profits to charitable causes.

During those dark years of 2001–2003, when energy prices were high and the country was experiencing a recession, Huntsman, along with the rest of the petrochemical industry, found itself in an overcapacity position. Every factor that could go wrong did, and we were on the financial precipice. Internally, I was discouraged, but I tried not to show it.

Few colleagues believed I could slay the economic dragons besieging us. One senior officer came to me and said that if I did not seek bankruptcy protection, he would have to leave the company. His expression in favor of bankruptcy didn't bother me. He was there, after all, to offer advice, which he did. He took it a step further when he said he would have to leave Huntsman if I did not follow the route he recommended. He no longer shared my values. When that occurs with an advisor or officer, we part ways—as we did in this case.

In every walk of life, we must believe we can succeed or, by definition, we already have failed. If a member of your team no longer believes you can attain success, that person—or you—should leave.

Those closest to you emotionally—a spouse, a child, or a parent—often can be a trusted advisor, for they know you best. That is particularly true with my wife, Karen. Whereas I tend to make

> *...we must believe we can succeed or, by definition, we already have failed.*

decisions from the heart, she makes them from the head. They are sound, logical, nonemotional approaches to problems. She also is more skeptical than I am. She has watched too many people take advantage of me, too many good deeds punished.

I often introduce Karen as the chairman of the chairman—a title *Forbes* bestowed on her in 1988—and there is nothing facetious about it. She knows her mind and tells it straight. (The children affectionately refer to her as "Queen Mother.")

Karen was about the only other person who resolutely believed from the beginning that we could pull the company out of the fire in the financial crisis of 2001–2003.

❖

There are no exact duplicates in nature. Each human is unique. When we seek to be like the next person, we lose autonomy. Failure often is the result of following the crowd. If the character of the person we are following lacks strength, honesty, and courage, that person's weaknesses can become ours. Conversely, following someone who exhibits those attributes reinforces one's own resolve and character.

> *Each human is unique. When we seek to be like the next person, we lose autonomy.*

You may find this odd, but when hiring managers, I never ask to see their GPAs or inquire as to their class standings. I don't care to know their academic majors. Be assured, I examine a person's background, but only for signs of integrity, commitment, and courage. I want to know the character of the person I am about to put at my side, and it's not hard to spot.

Applicants get points for holding full- or part-time jobs while in high school and college. It says something about one's commitment if he or she has had to underwrite part or all of their educational costs in achieving a degree.

During my White House stint, I answered to and interacted daily with Chief of Staff H.R. (Bob) Haldeman. It took only a few months before I began to notice the amoral atmosphere along "King's Row," as the West Wing was starting to be called. Everyone wanted to please Haldeman, no matter what the cost. His management style solicited only the type of information that would win grudging approval. No inner-staffer member said, "Wait a minute, Bob, this is wrong."

Haldeman often did not pick subordinates wisely because he selected aides who would be unquestioning in their service to the president, and the chief of staff determined just what that service would be. Potential legal problems, ethical challenges, and errors of judgment either were submerged or denied. That I was not one of the boys puzzled Haldeman and his immediate staff.

One evening, Haldeman invited his team to join him for dinner on the presidential yacht, *Sequoia*, a heady experience for a young assistant. It was a lovely night as we cruised down the Potomac. Aboard were Chuck Colson, Alex Butterfield, John Dean, Jeb Magruder, Ron Ziegler, and Dwight Chapin, most of whom would soon become household names.

Toward the end of dinner, about the time we were being served baked Alaska, Haldeman inquired of the assembled: "What are we going to do about Jon who works all day and doesn't play?" I was embarrassed. "Do you think there is any way we can get Huntsman out of his office to socialize with the rest of us?" he rhetorically asked the group.

It was a joke and it wasn't. He had made light of my propensity to keep my nose to the grindstone, but he was also sending a message. He had been trying to pull me into his inner circle for several months. So far, I had refused the lure. I attended meetings and carried out my responsibilities, but kept my distance and independence. I did not dislike any of them, not even Haldeman. Some I genuinely admired; a few I even respected. We spent 14 to 16 hours a day working together. We were a family, of sorts.

At the end of the day, I didn't want to play with these guys. I didn't like the rules under which many of them operated. I had different ideas about what counted in life. My lifestyle was less complex, not like those who sat around the table that night. Haldeman expected me to become one of his boys. I wouldn't do it.

I have always held in high regard individuals who informed me that certain behavior or policies were inappropriate. I respect candor. My door is always open for news—good or bad. Many leaders only want to hear the positive. It is dangerous to be employed by such people. Those who never want to hear bad news don't want to know when they are off course.

> *Many leaders only want to hear the positive. It is dangerous to be employed by such people.*

That, sadly, is the reason the news media is so full of stories about whistleblowers, individuals who usually are neither disloyal nor disgruntled employees. They were frustrated about an internal warning system that wasn't operational or valued. Higher-ups didn't want to hear bad news.

❖

Each of us starts with an ability to be a moral leader. From parents to CEOs, we possess the wisdom to see and appreciate the ethical, decent course. It is courage that separates those with wisdom from those who commit that wisdom to action. It is courage, and not the title, that separates genuine leaders from the pretenders.

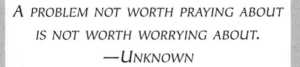

*A PROBLEM NOT WORTH PRAYING ABOUT
IS NOT WORTH WORRYING ABOUT.
—UNKNOWN*

*I AM AN OLD MAN AND HAVE
KNOWN A GREAT MANY TROUBLES,
BUT MOST OF THEM NEVER HAPPENED.
—MARK TWAIN*

CHAPTER EIGHT

GET MAD, NOT EVEN

Revenge is unhealthy and unproductive.
Learn to move on.

In the years following the 2000 election, Al Gore always looked mad. He constantly seemed upset. I suspect he continued to smart over the fact that he received more popular votes than rival George Bush, but the Electoral College vote went to Bush after the Supreme Court ruled Bush had won Florida.

Many of us are like that. We have been injured emotionally at one time or another, in one way or another—hurt by family, friends, business colleagues, news media, politicians, whatever—and the bitter urge to strike back becomes our first reaction.

We want to do what Ensign Pulver did in the movie *Mister Roberts*. He tossed a large, homemade firecracker into the ship's laundry room as payback for the ship's captain making Lt. Robert's life miserable.

There is a better, more productive route, although it can be emotionally difficult. The instructions are simple: Move on. Figure that this, too, shall pass. And Al Gore did just that, winning the Nobel Peace Prize for his work on global warming.

Put things behind you. Forget about replacing lost money, ignore a competitor's below-the-belt blow, never try to second-guess cancer. Accept what has transpired and move ahead in a positive and dignified way. I was hit with cancer three times, but I don't dwell on it.

Many years ago, a businessman I knew experienced a failed merger with his company. Consequently, he was forced to sell his business to another bidder at a lower return to the shareholders than the original deal would have realized. In his mind, he lost face.

He became determined to get even, no matter what the cost. The thought of a payback was all consuming. If the name of the company in the initial merger negotiation was ever mentioned, even in casual conversation, he exploded. If his friends had dealings with this institution, he tried to penalize them. It seemed his life's pursuit was to get even.

His personality changed. A naturally bright leader, his focus was no longer where it could do the most good. So much competence, passion, and drive wasted. Many of his friends found it difficult to be around him. He forgot to move on. The only person bitterness bites is the one who holds the grudge.

Grudges are physically, emotionally, and mentally draining, if not unhealthy. Being driven by revenge affects our hearts and blood pressure. Some scientists at the Huntsman Cancer Institute have developed theories that suggest this type of high-stress emotion might even induce cancer at an earlier stage than it might otherwise surface.

> *Grudges are physically, emotionally, and mentally draining, if not unhealthy.*

Unproductive emotions are potholes in the road to progress. They limit one's ability to move forward, to focus, to think positively, to make correct decisions, to act creatively. Time and productivity are wasted.

To not react to low blows, slights, and petty name-calling may require more willpower than humans can muster. Don't hold back when it comes to emotions. Let your feelings come out. Getting mad for a brief time is far better than a long and costly plan to get even. Make your reaction fast, furious, and finite. Vent your hurt, your anger, your frustrations. Let emotions rip. Then say to yourself: "There, I feel better. It's over. Move on."

If you are like me, you need to come to grips with a keen sensitivity to criticism. We have a subsequent need to justify, to explain, and to righteously deny in the face of accusations. Many years ago, I concluded that service to the community or to government earns a certain level of criticism—in the press, from the envious, or out of the mouths of adversaries. Face the future with the words of one of America's most criticized public figures ever, Richard Nixon: "Adversity introduces a man to himself."

Revenge is counterproductive. Besides, all bloodbaths eventually cease, if for no other reason than adversaries collapsing from exhaustion. Some even seek to restore old relationships. The ultimate payback, in any case, is your success. If a business competitor has caused you emotional injury, channel your energies into earning a bigger market share and

The ultimate payback is your success.

making your company more profitable. If it is a political slight, campaign harder to garner more votes than your opponent.

Doing better is the healthful response to most anything. In any walk of life, a positive, upbeat outlook trumps adversarial acts. Overlook trivial annoyances and imperfections of others. Hopefully, they will do the same with you.

There are times when it is prudent to turn the other cheek, especially when it comes to spouses, family members, and friends. Courtesy and love are contagious and are far more effective over the long haul than trying to ruin the reputation and well-being of another.

It pays to be positive and upbeat around your opposition. Attempting to get even or waging a

Those who plant mean, vengeful, and unjust seeds will reap what they sow. We tend to become what we degrade.

campaign of nastiness frequently backfires. Those who plant mean, vengeful, and unjust seeds will reap what they sow. We tend to become what we degrade.

On one occasion during my son's successful 2004 campaign for governor, I approached his primary-election opponent to wish him well. His supporters had been particularly negative toward Jon Jr. during the campaign. Staff members and volunteers surrounded their candidate. They looked uptight. I shook hands with each one and individually complimented them for the job they were doing. I inquired about their careers.

As I left the building, one of them followed me outside. Privately, he complimented me for being magnanimous and interested in their well-being. He inquired about the possibility of switching to my son's campaign.

When we get riled, we ought to simply vent to a trusted associate. Don't internalize it, but keep emotional displays brief because they are stressful to those around you. Working out feelings helps one from falling into the revenge mode. Don't waste months or years brooding over and plotting how to get even. Obsessing on grudges keeps them alive; forgiveness forces them to die. Moving on gets you back to business.

In reality, getting even is a form of self-pity. I view self-pity as one of the worst human weaknesses, a virus that can incapacitate otherwise decent, effective people. My employer in the first business in which I worked was always in a rage over competitors. We were in the egg-processing business. He continually schemed on how to make the competition fail. He wasted so much effort on this mission that his company suffered.

He insisted his staff fabricate stories about the competition with the news media. He concocted every negative thought and trick possible to make his competitors stumble. He died a pathetic, virtually bankrupt individual.

His bitterness overflowed to his children. No good came of it. He didn't even affect the other companies, which had simply ignored him and concentrated on expanding their own businesses.

Today, one of his competitors is the largest in its field. The owners are billionaires. My ex-employer is six feet underground and long forgotten.

Odds run against successfully achieving revenge. Attempting it wastes time and causes friction with those we love and who care most about us. Prayer is helpful for many people who can't seem to rid themselves of a grudge. It is soothing and permits forgiveness as well as the strength to move on. It allows a higher order to lend a hand, a being more knowledgeable than mortals.

Although many religions toy with the notion of selected vengeance, including the Old Testament eye-for-an-eye concept, forgiveness is a larger, more central theme. In Eastern religions, for example, it is believed that holding a grudge restrains one from moving forward on his or her spiritual journey.

Prayer to whomever or whatever you perceive to be your deity is good therapy.

Prayer to whomever or whatever you perceive to be your deity is good therapy. It is a source of renewal and strength. Besides, it's impossible for me to remain angry when I pray. Talk through your anger and move on without rancor, for bitterness ruins all of life's beauty.

Resentment underscores every person's weakness. Battling internal demons can flatten otherwise wonderful blessings. Hate does not fit well in the human heart. What's more, much of what we worry about and most of what we are angry about are imagined. It's the result of mounting anxiety in our souls. Why turn one mistake into two?

Don't concern yourself with avenging personal putdowns or injuries. Justice has a way of catching up to those who do injury to others. It happens most often without our assistance. A personal example:

Justice has a way of catching up to those who do injury to others. It happens most often without our assistance.

During the late 1980s, Huntsman Chemical was growing rapidly and looking for ways to diversify. Sweetheart Plastics, at the time America's largest producer of confectionary equipment—straws, paper cups and plates, and the like—was in our acquisition crosshairs because its products used vast amounts of polystyrene and polypropylene products Huntsman manufactured. Sweetheart Plastics was represented by an aggressive New York investment-banking firm.

My team and I had negotiated late into the night, finally crafting an $800 million deal for the company. When we formally presented it, the chief negotiator for the investment bank stated: "To ensure that you are the highest bidder for Sweetheart, you must raise your offer to $900 million. As you know, Jon, we have other options."

I was flabbergasted—not to mention upset. We had been discussing a sale in the $800 million range and had cobbled together the financing to make an offer of that magnitude. The investment bankers were bluffing—and lying. I called a timeout.

I returned to the meeting at midnight to announce we would not pay a penny more than the $800 million agreed upon. Sweetheart was fully priced and the deal could be transacted quickly.

"Think about it, Jon," repeated the negotiator, "$900 million and the business is yours."

I walked out and never returned. I was furious, but I moved on. The next highest bid for Sweetheart was $660 million, from an internal management team that neither knew how to operate the business nor had put together the proper financial package. It ended up far from being a sweetheart deal.

Greed cost the financial institution $140 million and a lawsuit from Sweetheart's bondholders. *Forbes* and *The Wall Street Journal* published stories about it. Within two years, Sweetheart sold again, this time for $445 million. Eventually, shareholders were left with 50 percent of the original offer.

I rest my case.

❖

The genesis of Richard Nixon's political demise was his inability to move on. He held grudges. He felt compelled to get even. Whether dark paranoia over so-called "enemies" or wrestling with old ghosts, it brought him down and altered history.

I often wondered if, in a small way, I could have changed any of that by working on Nixon's mindset.

Up close and without the benefit of hindsight or historic perspective, it was difficult for me at the time to detect how deep and sociopathic was his contempt for selected politicians, special interest groups, and members of the news media.

We assume that successful or revered people do not carry around demons like the rest of us. They do. When it comes to grudges, we all have held on to some for too long. What separates winners from losers is how fast we banish those demons.

Pay attention to that voice inside that says: Life is short. Move on. Step lively.

You cannot do a kindness too soon, for you never know how soon it will be too late.
—*Ralph Waldo Emerson*

Travel is fatal to prejudice, bigotry and narrow-mindedness... Broad, wholesome, charitable views of men and things cannot be acquired by vegetating in one little corner of the earth all one's life.
—*Mark Twain*

CHAPTER NINE

GRACIOUSNESS IS NEXT TO GODLINESS

*Treat competitors, colleagues,
employees, and customers with respect.*

Few human traits are as critical to one's relationship with others as graciousness. It embodies love, kindness, sensitivity, and charity—the qualities of people who have great inner faith. One's capacity to be kind, decent, and thoughtful is the manifestation of godliness, a demeanor that has earned respect for men and women of all faiths and backgrounds.

We are taught in our youth to be kind to others as a matter of habit. The lesson doesn't always stick around in adulthood. Decency is lacking in today's highly competitive business world, political arenas, and sporting events. It doesn't have to be. You can win with grace and decency. Winning with class is not a definition at odds with itself.

Perhaps some people are born with gracious genes and take to kindness more readily than others, but like golf, we can all give it a try. I use the words *kind*, *gracious*, and *charitable* synonymously, even though dictionaries parse their definitions. I notice that "benevolence" shows up in describing all three words. They are close enough for me because all three require a substantial degree of warmth and genuineness.

> *Perhaps some people are born with gracious genes and take to kindness more readily than others, but like golf, we can all give it a try.*

My mother could never bring herself to speak unkindly of others. She was gracious to one and all, believing there is no inner difference between white and black, Christian and Hindu, male and female, rich and poor. We were all God's children, each to be treated with love and respect. My mother never gave a sermon on being gracious, never wrote an essay on the subject, never even discussed it in a formal sense. She simply lived kindness every day of her life—which, of course, is the most effective example of all. Francis of Assisi's powerful line, "Preach the Gospel, and if you must, use words," comes to mind.

Her life was a textbook model that I have tried to follow, notwithstanding obvious shortcomings. Kathleen Robison Huntsman was born and raised knowing that kindness is a priority to be followed throughout one's life. Her father was much the same way. It pained Grandfather Robison to charge anyone for services rendered. (More on his charity in Chapter 12, "The Bottom Line.") Obviously, he did not get rich, but everybody loved him. His heart and motives were pure. My mother learned much from her father and I from my grandfather.

I know of no truly successful person who does not demonstrate a sense of decency. There are those who appear successful on the surface, but who in reality are selfish, unhappy individuals lacking the motivation and capacity to love. It's a shame they never experience the joy of being kind to others.

During my senior year at Palo Alto High School, I was elected student body president. My campaign platform sought to give every student attention and recognition. I had numerous opportunities to practice what I preached, but one instance stands out above the others.

Ron Chappel was a classmate. Disfigured and with an artificial leg, he looked emaciated and lonely. He always sat by himself in the corner of the cafeteria when not in class. I had noticed him, of course, but made little effort to engage him in conversation. For whatever reason, I one day got up from my table of friends and walked over to Ron's table. I sat down and struck up a conversation.

I continued that routine for a week. Gradually, others joined us. Ron's table became the "in" place in the cafeteria. We expanded his inclusion to social activities and athletics. He became our team manager. His senior year became the best year of his life. The following year, I was brokenhearted when his mother told me that he had passed away.

Karen and I have been blessed with nine children who, in turn, have given us, at this writing, 56 grandchildren. Our family is the crown jewel of

Karen's and my lives. Our children love one another; they are competitive yet get along famously.

Our youngest son, Mark, who was born in 1975, has severe mental limitations. The doctor told us he would never read, write, or be able to attend school, that his age would permanently be that of a four-year-old. We were devastated at the news, as most parents would be, yet over the years he has taught us much.

Mark doesn't know one's background or station in life. Whether one is a Democrat or a Republican, earns minimum wage or $10 million a year, or attends church on Sunday carries little standing with him. The company custodian and CEO are held in the same esteem. Mark judges only the goodness of the person's heart. In that, he can size up individuals quickly. If their heart is good, he gives them a big hug.

He is not easily fooled in this regard. One cannot be insincere and be considered a friend by Mark. He spots phoniness immediately. Although he talks with a limited vocabulary, Mark communicates effectively. His friends are numerous. They are individuals who have the ability to signal the purity of their hearts, their graciousness, and their kindness.

Many would say there is no place for graciousness and the Golden Rule in business, politics, athletics, or other highly competitive settings. Only results count. I would join Mark in saying hogwash! How we treat others will be our epitaphs.

Having spoken at hundreds of funerals in my lifetime, I have discovered that final remarks relate a great deal about the deceased. It would be a fascinating experience to hear, in advance, what will be said in our eulogy. Few words are wasted over one's academic achievements, professional career, or wealth. Families receive major play, but the most spotlighted characteristic is how the dearly departed treated others.

It would do us each well to think about what might be said at our eulogies. Would it be similar to how we see ourselves? And what will be mentioned in those informal "eulogies" delivered in the neighborhood, the workplace, and whispered in the pews following your demise?

Every day, our eulogies are being written. When they finally are presented, we obviously will be in no physical shape to offer a rebuttal. Today—

right now—begin working toward a reputation for graciousness. Only you can shape the content of your forthcoming eulogy.

Every day, our eulogies are being written.

Businesses, too, have reputations. Many companies are known for their values, customer and employee relations, innovative spirit, and philanthropic endeavors. The recent downfalls of Enron, Tyco, WorldCom, and other such notables have reminded us that deception, greed, and sundry indecencies also are present in the misty corporate world.

I once had the pleasure to be in the presence of the Dalai Lama. He made a meaningful observation: "Accumulation of wealth for the sake of wealth alone is self-defeating. Only in seeing one's work as a calling, a means to serve a higher purpose, can we find true fulfillment."

On another occasion, he said: "Relate to others with warmth, human affection, honesty, and compassion." Thoughtful advice.

Most companies and individuals seek success and respect. To reach these goals requires a sense of compassion for others and a desire to make others happy. Happiness is so meaningful to our lives. It often comes to us when we try to make others happy. Graciousness is catching.

In his book, *There Is No Such Thing as Business Ethics*, John Maxwell maintains that in today's marketplace, 70 percent of the people who leave their jobs do so because they do not feel valued. That's an indictment of how shabbily many executives and directors treat employees. Everyone wants to be valued, to know that they count. People need to be appreciated, trusted, and respected in every segment of their lives.

Maxwell holds that only one rule is necessary in governing ethical decision making: the Golden Rule. Treating competitors, the community, employees, and fellow humans with the same courtesies we would like shown to us works for me.

There is a practical side to decent behavior, too. Customers, employers, and suppliers are people who understand and appreciate civility and graciousness. They normally react in kind, and that can be good for profits. Bottom lines would be better served if we put this philosophy into practice.

How would I like to be treated in this situation? That's all you need to ask yourself in most instances.

The Golden Rule is a guideline of life in every culture I know. Many people are familiar with the "do unto others" admonition of the New Testament. It may surprise you to know how similarly the world's religions view this concept.

Confucianism states: "Do not do to others what you would not like yourself." Zoroastrians are advised that "if you do not wish to be mistreated by others, do not mistreat anyone yourself." Muslims are taught no one is a true believer "until he desires for his brother that which he desires for himself." Hinduism warns never to behave "towards others in a way which is disagreeable to oneself." The Torah says: "What is hateful to you, do not do to your neighbor. This is the whole Torah; all the rest is commentary. Go and learn it."

There are other ways to look at the Golden Rule. My late oil-baron friend, Armand Hammer, was a controversial world figure for most of the 20th century because of his close relationship with the Soviet Union. He believed we could more effectively deal with Communist nations through trade rather than by rattling sabers.

He and I traveled together to the old Soviet Union several times. His stories are legendary—some even true. Nevertheless, during our initial meeting in his Beverly Hills headquarters, I noticed the sign on the wall behind his desk: "The Golden Rule: He who controls the gold, makes the rules."

That is not my approach.

We all know people who we love to be around. They provide us with inspiration and joy. My friend Mark Rose is one of those people. I have never heard him say a negative word about another person. Forever smiling and positive, he never talks about himself. Others are the center of his focus. As a result, he is at peace with himself.

Gracious people make a real difference in our lives. Unfortunately, so do people who embody self-pity, arrogance, and self-importance. They don't listen. Most are talking so rapidly about themselves, they seldom learn anything new.

I have discovered in my dealings with the U.S. Congress that good listeners are rare. Elected officials live in a Beltway bubble where they are caught up in their own sense of importance. They communicate in babble-speak. It is that kind of atmosphere that has led to the contentious and bitter relations between Republicans and Democrats.

I hold in high esteem those peacemakers and statesmen who maintain a sense of humility, kindness, and graciousness. A number of such noble souls still reside on Capitol Hill, but I fear they are becoming an endangered species. Thankfully, there are signs that some alarmed politicians are realizing this and are attempting to forge a new, more civilized and respectful political atmosphere that would better serve our nation's interest.

In 2003, *Parents* magazine conducted a survey on the qualities that parents most wanted to instill in their offspring. The resounding winners were good manners and religious faith. And by manners, these parents reported they meant behavior involving other people, respecting others, and being considerate.

It is not much of a surprise that, of all vocations, the most decent and gracious people are found in religious settings. The now deceased heads of two religions—LDS Church President Gordon B. Hinckley and Pope John Paul II—immediately stand out for me.

In the early 1990s, I met the late John Paul II at the Vatican in a meeting arranged by Roger Cardinal Mahony of Los Angeles. (At the time, I, a tithe-paying, devout Mormon, was the second biggest donor to the Catholic charities in the Diocese of Salt Lake City.) The pope took my hand and thanked me for my help to the needy. "I have never met a Mormon before," he said. "I want to compliment you on all you do to help others."

I found myself momentarily speechless, not to mention a bit teary, but I managed to respond: "I have never met Your Holiness before, either, and wish to convey my love to you in the same manner." He knows so well what kindness to others brings. He is one of my heroes.

My own church leader, President Gordon Hinckley, who was a close friend for more than three decades, too, was a wise leader with a remarkable sense of graciousness. He began nearly every personal conversation with a compliment. I can understand why he, too, is so beloved. He has been my role model, as has his successor, Thomas S. Monson, another close friend, who was sustained as president and prophet in 2008.

While I learned a basic value system from those closest to me as a child, my church has provided me with a continuous source of renewal of those principles. When attempting to play life's games by the rules, it helps not to compartmentalize family, faith, and career.

> *When attempting to play life's games by the rules, it helps not to compartmentalize family, faith, and career.*

❖

No one lives or dies unto himself. In his day, Andrew Carnegie made 38 other men millionaires. That sort of financial fallout has continued down to the present day with the successes of large businesses, including my own, enriching others. Conversely, when businesses go broke, they tend to drag down others with them. Employees lose jobs, suppliers lose business, and creditors lose money.

Each of us has a stake in the accomplishments and failures of those around us; each of us holds an interest in the deeds of others. When one person beautifies a neighborhood, the entire community is

Each of us has a stake in the accomplishments and failures of those around us; each of us holds an interest in the deeds of others.

enhanced. When a CEO trips, stakeholders stumble. Like the tide that raises all ships, no one can lift others without first being made better himself.

I have always treasured the handwritten notes and personal calls that have come during times of emotional or physical stress. Somehow, such expressions seem more personal and meaningful than an e-mail.

Captains of industry, successful CEOs and managers, political leaders of depth, religious hierarchy, and effective parents take advantage of personal communication when expressing support or appreciation—and they usually don't wait for a crisis situation.

Our company has more than a hundred manufacturing, distribution, and sales offices around the globe. I love to visit our facilities, even though I don't know how to operate the equipment and don't understand the chemical formulas for our products (although I am still a pretty good salesperson). I leave that to the experts. What I embrace are the people.

Employee relations are at the center of successful businesses. Labor develops a bad attitude toward management when executives spend more time at the country club than in the manufacturing plants. Top officials of companies big and small must find opportunities to go from employee to employee, thanking each one and acknowledging individual contributions.

Research suggests a link between the lack of civility and violence. Nearly two million acts of violence on some level occur in the American workplace annually, primarily by people who believe management or colleagues slighted them.

Leaders must instill in others a sense of entitlement, appreciation, and loyalty. If one does this successfully, others are lifted to greater achievements. Let me assure you, watching dreams unfold is one of the great joys of leadership.

I identify with the words of Thomas Jefferson when, in the Declaration of Independence, he wrote:

...watching dreams unfold is one of the great joys of leadership.

"In the support of this Declaration, we mutually pledge to each other our lives, our fortunes and our sacred honor." It was clear to Jefferson that every man and woman shared in the successes of others. For Jefferson, mutual support was essential.

On many occasions, I have recited from John Donne's poem, "No Man Is an Island." It brings hope and joy into my life. Indulge me two verses:

No man is an island,
No man stands alone;
Each man's joy is joy to me,
Each man's grief is my own.

We need one another,
So I will defend
Each man as my brother,
Each man as my friend.

If we could but express these remarkable words to one another in our homes, in our places of worship, in our businesses, and in our associations, peace would abide in our souls, and the world would indeed be a better place.

NONE OF US IS AS SMART AS ALL OF US.
—JAPANESE PROVERB

GIVE ME A CHILD FOR THE FIRST SEVEN YEARS, AND YOU MAY DO WHAT YOU LIKE WITH HIM AFTERWARD.
—A JESUIT MAXIM

CHAPTER TEN

YOUR NAME IS
ON THE DOOR

*Operate businesses and organizations
as if they're family owned.*

My brother Blaine and I started the family business in 1970. Huntsman remained a family-owned and-operated company for 35 years, eventually becoming the largest in America. Early in 2005, we decided to go public as a way to reduce debt with new capital and increase Karen's and my philanthropy. My family continued to run Huntsman Corp. in a similar manner as we did when the corporation was privately owned because it still carried our name.

Although we are going down this new road with the best of intentions, it saddens me that today's ownership complexities or a need for additional capital eventually forces many family businesses to face the same decision. This does not mean family enterprises will cease to exist or that change is necessarily a bad thing, but it does cause me some anxiety.

The family is the basic societal unit. As such, it is the foundation for society's prosperity, order, happiness, and values. Business is much the same as families. These same aspirations should be found in business "families" as well. This can be more easily accomplished when the business is family-owned, but the wise CEO of a publicly traded company will operate as if his or her last name is on the company marquee.

Some families are large, others are small, and some are untraditional, but it is in this setting that one's greatest education is experienced, where fundamental, life-long values are learned. It is not hard to understand why the home is my focus and that key decisions in Huntsman Corp. have been made within the family circle.

Wealth and power are thought by many to be a formula for family divisiveness. This is not necessarily the case. I saw my grandparents' six children squabble over a $30,000 estate. Riches have little to do with family cohesiveness.

Each of our children, in his or her own way, has experienced the heartaches, pain, and challenges of our business. They have been astute students of life. They have known from the start there is no such thing as a Midas touch. The realities of this world are hard work, preparation, negotiation, determination, commitment, honesty, and charity.

Where appropriate, the workplace should be an extension of the family, a place where an appreciation for decency, respect, and basic values are encouraged, and examples of proper moral behavior are the rule.

Jay Kenfield Morley's description of life sums up how critical it is for the workplace to be an extension of the home: "The recipe for happiness is to have just enough money to pay the monthly bills you acquire, a little surplus to give you confidence, a little too much work each day, enthusiasm for your work, a substantial share of good health, a couple of real friends, and a wife and children to share life's beauty with you."

My father was a rural schoolteacher in Idaho. Our first two-room home required a 40-foot walk to the outhouse, an unpleasant undertaking in the winter, but typical for a rural family in the late 1930s.

Eventually, my dad went off to World War II like so many other fathers of this era. When he returned, we built a small home in Pocatello, Idaho. A few years later, we moved to California so he could get his doctorate at Stanford. Our residence for three years was in a campus Quonset hut that was divided into 16 "apartments," each approximately 600 square feet in size and separated by walls made of heavy cardboard. With my parents and two brothers, the quarters were cramped and embarrassing for a teenager, but it was home.

In 1959, I married my sweetheart, Karen, and we subsequently had three daughters and six sons. Our home has been a place of comfort, love, and tranquility. I know not all homes in the world are like this. I have observed in my travels many difficult and trying domestic situations where housing is pitifully inadequate. Families live in boxes, tin shacks, tents, or other makeshift arrangements. It is emotionally difficult to visit such places.

I emphasize in employee meetings that families come first. I have insisted our company workplaces attempt to be an extension of a supportive home. Too many put career advancement and accumulation of wealth ahead of family, rationalizing they will get around to the family next year. Next year never comes. And soon it is too late—for the family, for fulfillment, and for success.

During a recent visit to one of our plant sites in Scarlino, Italy, I underscored to employees that their foremost concern in life was not their jobs, but their families. They listened intently through an interpreter and appeared pleased by their employer's positive expressions about the family. When I finished, they stood and applauded. A cynic might say they did so to impress the boss, that they would have cheered if I had read them Shakespeare. I don't think so. Those employees appeared deeply touched as I went from one to another, giving small hugs or handshakes.

When I recently gave a similar speech in Malaysia, all 800 employees clapped and seemed pleased. They love their children just as much as I love mine. Their families are as high a priority to them as mine is to me. They understood precisely what I was saying and why I was saying it.

The same is true in China, South Africa, Armenia, Australia, or in any of the many countries where Huntsman has manufacturing or distribution operations. It makes no difference where one lives.

> *It makes no difference where one lives. Everyone wants to feel noticed, respected, and valued.*

Everyone wants to feel noticed, respected, and valued. Unfortunately, large corporations tend to be run by the book. They frequently are perceived by employees to be sterile and uncaring. Running a business as if you own it prompts a more personal touch.

Employees want to be assured the owner or CEO truly cares about them. How can one convince employees they are valued if their families are omitted from that concern?

Most employees like to hear directly from the owner or head of a company. The first thing I underscore is their preeminent responsibility to families and loved ones. If there is success within the walls of our homes, we will do better in our vocational pursuits. We work safer in a happier work environment. If we are at peace in our personal lives, we are more successful and find more satisfaction in our work.

Karen and I started including our children in the discussion of the family business as early as elementary school, but we insisted on two rules:

> **Rule 1:** *In a family business, check your ego at the door. There is no room for self-aggrandizement or self-promotion. In a family business, everyone knows the abilities and shortcomings of the others.*
>
> *There are no secrets. The success of family businesses relies on trust, respect, and love.*
>
> **Rule 2:** *Be a cheerleader for each other. Seek good fortune for the other person first. Most family businesses end up in disarray because of the selfish interests of one or another sibling.*

Effective communication is essential. Parents must talk to each other openly and honestly about the business—and especially about estate planning. Parents must educate their children in those areas. Secret wills and selective entitlements upon a death almost always result in family feuds or lawsuits.

I assured my children, even after most of them started working in the family business, that I am a parent first and chairman of the board second. Family enterprises career off the road when parents place business ahead of parental nurturing.

❖

Employees must be treated as equals. When a company is financially successful, it ought to share its bounty with employees, the community, and customers the same as it does with owners or stockholders. The marketplace appears to be getting less considerate on this point, with the obvious exception of pay packages for top management, which have been increasing four to five times faster than compensation for their rank-and-file employees.

Whether one runs a family business or is CEO of a public company, ways must be identified to recognize and give credit to others—at all levels of the organization. The surest path to success is one where others walk with you. Plants and equipment can be replaced easily; hard-working, loyal employees are as valuable as precious gems. They are critical to any leadership success. If CEOs are the mind of the organization, employees are the heart. The corporate culture is the soul.

When unethical or immoral behavior occurs within an organization, be it a business, charity, church, or team, it greatly impacts everyone, similar to the effect a prodigal son or an unfaithful spouse has on a family.

If top executives fail to follow their moral compasses, how can one expect those they lead to adhere to moral values? And if employees in the *The surest path to success is one where others walk with you.* workplace do not care about ethics or morality, how can they expect their children to be any different? Everyone loses.

That's why it is especially critical that employees understand the company's values. Employees ought to know, for instance, that a corporation's culture dictates that a sizable portion of the profits is to be returned to society, and why. They must understand the true measure of success, for them individually as well as the company, is not only how much one acquires, but also how much one gives back.

❖

I remember visiting a Huntsman plant in eastern Canada several years ago. I had just left a church meeting, and my thoughts were centered more around the message I had just heard than what I was going to say to our people, so I opened by reminding them that we walk by faith, not by sight.

I explained that if we had faith in fellow human beings, there would be fewer accidents and safety violations. If we had faith in each other, brotherly love and joyous association would follow. If we each had true faith, we would not need sight. We would be lifted up by loved ones and would become stronger and more effective people. We would not display self-pity or extravagances. Our needs would be met.

When I finished, I realized I had not mentioned a word about the company's productivity, costs, or sales. In a way, though, what I said indirectly covered those operating areas. Realistic goals are achieved when those responsible for meeting them are committed.

Moreover, everyone wants to know the true feelings and heartstrings of their leaders, along with news on how the organization is faring. In truth, though, you can't get a good read on the organization without knowing the feelings of the person who is leading it.

The climate created by a CEO and his or her management team has more impact on employees than we generally realize. People bring out the best in themselves when they hear and see the best in their leaders.

Over the years, we have given out thousands of scholarships to the children of our employees. It has been a joy to meet many of these students and to receive invitations to their high school or college graduations. When we become a part of the employees' families, morale is at its highest. Who isn't excited when their children succeed? And when someone is feeling good, his or her workplace productivity shows it.

❖

As Huntsman Corp. begins its new chapter as a publicly traded company, some of the family atmosphere may well disappear. Many public shareholders aren't as altruistic as they ought to be because they only want a quick return on their investment. That's a pity. The greatest dividends are those paid to hard-working men and women through bonuses, gifts, scholarships, and praise. Public or private, we still consider it a family business. After all, our name is on the door.

The greatest dividends are those paid to hardworking men and women through bonuses, gifts, scholarships, and praise.

All companies—public or private—must create a culture in which employees come first and are treated royally. Believe me, they always return the favor.

*FIND OUT HOW MUCH GOD HAS GIVEN
YOU AND FROM IT TAKE WHAT YOU NEED;
THE REMAINDER IS NEEDED BY OTHERS.*
—*ST. AUGUSTINE*

*WE ARE THE MERE TRUSTEES OF
WHAT FUNDS WE ARE TEMPORARILY
GIVEN ON THIS EARTH.
MAY WE SHARE THOSE WITH OTHERS.*
—*ANDREW CARNEGIE*

*A MAN WRAPPED UP IN HIMSELF
MAKES A VERY SMALL BUNDLE.*
—*BENJAMIN FRANKLIN*

CHAPTER ELEVEN

THE OBLIGATION TO GIVE BACK

*Nobody is completely self-made;
return the favors and good fortune.*

Giving is my favorite topic. I hardly know where to begin. Let's start with a disturbing revelation about a president I greatly admired and respected, Richard Nixon. As White House special assistant and staff secretary, I got to see details of his tax filings before the IRS returns were released to the public. In 1971, for instance, he gave only $500 to charity on a declared income in excess of $400,000. I was shocked. To me, that pittance was more onerous than Watergate.

Philanthropy ought to be the preeminent ingredient in everyone's recipe for material gain. No matter what the field, no star of any success story is a

No matter what the field, no star of any success story is a totally self-made man or woman.

totally self-made man or woman. Along the way, all of us received help from others; most of us also were the beneficiaries of lucky breaks. We all owe a portion of our success to others, incurring a debt in the process, and the only way to repay that assistance is by sharing your good fortune.

I get goose bumps thinking of the blessings that have come my way. It wasn't always so. For years, the shoe was on the other foot. People shared what they had with the Huntsman family. My uncle, grandfather, and mother taught me the art of giving.

Uncle Lon had only a sixth-grade education. A hardscrabble Utah farmer, he boasted of few possessions. When I turned eight, he gave me his pocket watch. It was one of those old-fashioned watches with the big hands and a chain. (Uncle Lon never wore a wristwatch, and I don't either.) I proudly took that timepiece to school. All day in that third-grade classroom, I would pull out that magnificent timepiece to check the hour. I couldn't believe I possessed such an amazing watch that once belonged to my favorite uncle.

A few years later, when my folks were struggling, Uncle Lon gave me a pair of his shoes. Mine had become somewhat scruffy. With Uncle Lon's shoes, I considered myself the best-dressed person in my class. Those farmer's shoes hardly were a fashion statement, but I didn't care. I adored them.

Mother had little in the way of material means, but she knew I loved lemon pies, especially those she made from scratch. In her mind, making a pie was the nicest tangible thing she could do for me. Every few days, a lemon pie would be waiting when I got home from school.

I mentioned my mother's dad, Grandfather Robison, in an earlier chapter. He owned a small motel in Fillmore, Utah, from the 1920s through the 1950s. The units in those pre-World War II days were individual cabins. Motorists would pay $3 to $4 a night to stay in a cabin. There was no inside plumbing. Bathrooms were located at the end of the small path behind the cabins. When Grandpa noticed a family was struggling financially, he would only charge them $1 a night. In many cases, when they would come to pay in the morning, he would tell them, "That's okay. Someday maybe you can return the favor to somebody else."

As kids, we all were taught to share and share alike. We garnered praise from grownups when we engaged in letting others play with our toys, especially the less fortunate. We quickly learned that generosity was among the highest attributes a person could acquire. Even as children, we frowned on stingy playmates.

By high school, the Huntsman family finances had worked their way up to a point they could barely be labeled modest. With my father enrolled in graduate school, everyone contributed to the common pot. My brother Blaine and I each held two jobs to help with medical expenses and the cost of keeping the family car running. I had no idea where I would go to college, but I hoped that somehow I would be able to attend a university that would be challenging and appropriate for my future.

During my senior year, Harold L. Zellerbach, head of the nation's second-largest paper company, came to our high school in Palo Alto. Accompanying him was Raymond Saalbach, director of admissions of The Wharton School at the

University of Pennsylvania. They were seeking a western states high school senior to be the recipient of the Zellerbach family scholarship to attend this prestigious business school.

I had never heard of Wharton. I did not know that it was the first business school in America, or that it was on its way to preeminent status worldwide. Mr. Zellerbach, among Wharton's most famous alumni, met with me to discuss the possibility of my attending with a scholarship—all because classes had been dismissed that day for a teacher's convention. I was student body president, and the principal had phoned me at home to invite me to meet with Mr. Zellerbach and Dr. Saalbach.

Based on that and my high school performance, I received the Wharton scholarship. I thanked the two men, but said the grant would not be sufficient to permit me to attend. I would have to work full-time to make it financially. I wasn't sure I could succeed academically in an Ivy League school when burdened with full-time employment.

They worked out a further arrangement whereby all of my tuition, fees, and room and board also would be covered. And thus I went off to Wharton, an experience that launched my career. I had been in

> *I had no idea how I would repay the Zellerbach family. They would not have let me, even if I were able. Instead, they simply said, pass it on.*

the right place at the right time and was thrust into a situation by those who, at the time, had more confidence in me than I had in myself. It was a life-altering break.

I had no idea how I would repay the Zellerbach family. The fact was I financially couldn't. They would not have let me, even if I were able. Instead, they simply said, in essence, pass it on. And I have tried. Thousands of scholarships have been given over the years to young people around the world.

❖

All religions of the world reserve a high place on their must-do lists for giving to the less fortunate. Christianity calls it *charity*; for Jews, it is *tzedaka*; Muslims have their *zakat*; Hindus their *bhakti*, to name but four examples.

Karen and I have given a portion of our paycheck to worthy causes every year since I was in the navy making $320 a month. For the past 20 years, we concentrated on making money so we could give it away.

Monetarily, the most satisfying moments in my life have not been the excitement of closing a great deal or the reaping of handsome profits from it. They have been when I was able to help others in need—especially "the least of these, my brethren." There's no denying that I am a deal junkie, but I also have developed an addiction for giving.

The more one gives, the better one feels; and the better one feels about it, the easier it becomes to give. It is a wonderfully warm, slippery slope. If you require a less-altruistic reason to give, try this: Philanthropy is plain good business. It energizes a company.

Philanthropy is plain good business. It energizes a company.

As a family-owned company, Huntsman Corp. did not answer to Wall Street, whose shortsighted greed often curtails public companies in their philanthropic responsibilities. In place of that push for ever-expanding profits, we had pressure—at times overbearing—to fulfill charitable commitments. That required more discipline than if we only had to meet Wall Street expectations. Once you make a commitment to charity, you must honor it.

Publicly owned companies are not exempt from the requisite of returning a portion of their profits to worthwhile causes. As chairman of Huntsman when it went public in 2005, I made sure those commitments were met. (As this revise is written, our worldwide company is in the process of selling to another chemical company. Proceeds from that sale will provide a billion-dollar foundation to ensure that the giving continues in perpetuity.)

As philanthropic commitments are completed, new ones are made. The giving bar is constantly being raised. A company's focus is clouded without such reaching. There were years when I gave away more money than I made. I simply told my managers that we have a higher goal and that we all would have to do better. My son Peter is fond of saying the challenge for Huntsman executives is making money as fast as I give it away.

In almost every human being, there is an inner desire to help others. Unfortunately, some of us never quite find the time or the reason. We delay giving until it is too late or until someone we love passes away or no longer is in need of our generosity. In other instances, giving can be tainted or have too many strings attached.

The Jewish philosopher Maimonides described eight levels of giving, ranging from that which is given grudgingly, insufficiently, or only when asked (the lowest forms) to giving where neither party knows the other's identity and helping a person to become self-sufficient (the two highest).

There is no more important human quality than sharing with others. There is no source of true happiness more complete than an act of charity. It is what life is all about. In bad economic times, I have had to take out bank loans to meet my philanthropic pledges. (Industrial downturns do not first consult with charitable obligations.)

My bankers questioned the prudence in borrowing money simply to turn around and give it to others. My response was simple. If we make commitments to help others, there ought to be no retreat from those obligations solely because the company's finances are not as temporarily robust as anticipated. I acknowledge, though, this is easier said than done. Our obligation to give back, however, is not erased during financially challenging times. The temptation to gather around you what money you have left is strong. Overcome it. The poor nearly always give a greater proportion of their disposable income than the wealthy.

It is of little consequence where or how or to whom we give. What really matters is our attitude.

It is of little consequence where or how or to whom we give. What really matters is our attitude.

I have listened to thousands of sermons on the urgent need to give. I find myself wondering why it is that preachers never talk about how much fun it is to give, or whether they are indeed doing with their personal resources what their sermons suggest.

Today, my philanthropic focus centers on one of the largest cancer research centers and hospitals in the world. It has taken enormous amounts of money to build this world-class facility. It was a joy beyond measure to witness the completion of the Huntsman Cancer Institute and Hospital in the summer of 2004. I am hopeful we can build additional cancer hospitals around the country in the future.

Every week, I try to bring cheer to our patients, hugging those undergoing chemotherapy. In many cases, their life is precarious. In all cases, they are scared. An embrace and a word of encouragement can be as beneficial as any medicine they will receive. My mother, father, and stepmother all died of cancer. I had cancer three times. It is difficult for me to not become emotional when I greet cancer patients.

Donations don't always have to be money. In many ways, time is more precious than dollars. Giving of one's time, lending one's stature, and providing one's expertise can be as meaningful as money. Leaders ought to set aside time for volunteer or public service work. A recent national survey ranks Minneapolis and Salt Lake City as America's two most volunteer-minded cities, but even those two blue ribbons represent

> *Donations don't always have to be money. In many ways, time is more precious than dollars.*

barely two in five adults engaging in periodic volunteer activities.

Wealth isn't always measured in dollar signs. We each have time, talent, and creativity, all of which can be powerful forces for positive change. Share those blessings in whatever form they come and to the level you have been blessed.

❖

At one time, I believed charitable giving was purely voluntary. About 25 years ago, I changed my mind. Giving back applies to everyone, but it surely is not optional, at least for the rich or for corporations. It is the moral obligation of any person of wealth or any business worthy of its name to return to the community some of what they have been given. We are but temporary trustees of our fortunes, no matter the size.

> *At one time, I believed charitable giving was purely voluntary. About 25 years ago, I changed my mind.*

No less a committed capitalist than Andrew Carnegie lectured the well-heeled in his 1889 work

The Gospel of Wealth to return their "surplus wealth to the mass of their fellows in the form best calculated to do them lasting good." And he set a remarkable example with his endowment of libraries around the nation.

Many wealthy people are under the erroneous belief that the true measure of financial success is not what you make but what you keep. They spend lifetimes working tax dodges and accounting schemes to pass along their good fortune to their children.

> *Many wealthy people are under the erroneous belief that the true measure of financial success is not what you make but what you keep.*

No question about it, one gauge of success is how much wealth one acquires in his or her lifetime. The more meaningful and lasting measurement, though, is how much one gives away.

My message is not solely for the fraternity of the rich. Nobody gets off the hook. If just the rich give, little changes. All must give their share. Be a benevolent overseer of your harvest for each of our stewardships is temporary. We have only a short time to see that wealth, however humble or vast, is spread about to worthy needs. Giving is a spiritual obligation.

The Christian gospel, for one, makes that mandate clear: If a man has two coats, should he not give one of them to the man who is without a coat? For Jews, charity is a duty centered on the belief that everything we own is God-given. One is obligated to share with those who do not have enough.

Giving to the poor is one of the Five Pillars of Islam. In most Islamic cultures, hoarding is considered wrong. Giving away surplus protects one from greed and envy. In fact, Islam encourages the practice of endowing money or property, called *waqf*, for the purpose of maintaining schools, hospitals, churches, and the like.

Save for God's grace (and a few worldly breaks), there go us.

All three religions are making the same point: Put back into society as much as you extract. Give generously to the less fortunate. Save for God's grace (and a few worldly breaks), there go us.

We don't need millions of dollars to live comfortably. Yet it is often the wealthiest citizens in our society who find it the most difficult to share, whereas those with little seem to be first in line to give what they have.

Sandra Lee Anderson died June 28, 2008, unnoticed outside of her family and circle of friends in the Spokane, Washington, area. I came across her obituary quite by chance. I did not know her, but I wished I had because her story is worth sharing by way of example. By all accounts, she was an outstandingly kind and generous person who lived on a fixed income and suffered from a multitude of health problems. She loved working with people who had developmental disabilities. Sandy Anderson tithed to a little-known church and thanked the Lord daily for her blessings. She always was there with a donation for those who were less fortunate than she. I believe there are many low-income men and women in the world who daily put to shame the many wealthy folks.

How much ought the wealthy render? I have given this considerable thought. There is no set formula, but I would hold that the excess over and above one's guidelines for a comfortable standard of living is a reasonable starting point. What is a desirable quality of life when it comes to shelter, food, medical care, clothing, transportation, entertainment, travel, and rainy-day funds? That's for each individual to figure out.

To squander the excess is selfish and foolish. Unprofitable investments and expensive toys will almost always be the byproduct of having more money than one needs.

Companies are under the same mandate to share as individuals, but simply to give because it is good for the company image or because material gain may result from trumpeting one's philanthropy carries this downside: The sense of social responsibility withers.

❖

Foundations and nonprofits get hit doubly hard during economic hard times. Not only are donations traditionally down, but these groups' investments are getting hammered. That means less grant money is available for worthy projects—just at a time when assistance is especially necessary. When donations are needed most, they are the hardest to come by.

Businesses often go through highs and lows, not unlike people. Recessions, energy crises, monetary setbacks, competitiveness, and marketplace potholes can mean difficult times for businesses. I remember and appreciate those individuals and institutions that stepped up in difficult times. I try to do business today with those who remembered us when we were down, the bankers who allowed us lines of credit in times of severe financial stress, suppliers who permitted us credit when profits had evaporated, and those who extended a helping hand along the way.

❖

Residents of Utah, according to the *Chronicle of Philanthropy*, are among the most generous folks in the nation, giving away up to 15 percent of their discretionary income each year. Much of that is the result of so many Utahns tithing for religious purposes.

The IRS may allow you to commingle secular and sectarian giving on your tax form, but I separate religious donations from public charity. Putting money in the collection basket, be it a weekly offering or annual tithing, is a good thing. It is a duty for individuals who practice a religion, but there are many other worthwhile causes.

Congregations regularly are reminded that donations are a requisite for an eternal reward. Without pulpit pressure, I doubt whether many religious institutions would collect the sums they do. It would be healthy for all of us, especially the wealthy, to experience that same sort of collection-plate pressure when it comes to secular philanthropy.

> *True giving is doing something for somebody who can never repay you.*

True giving is doing something for somebody who can never repay you. Sharing wealth and kindness, embracing those in need, and creating opportunities for others are a societal duty. The only thing that changes as we move through life is the scope of our giving.

You don't have to be a billionaire to be a philanthropist. The first definition the *Oxford Dictionary* provides for *philanthropy* is "a love of humankind."

All that is required to be a philanthropist is a passion for making a difference.

And did I mention it is great fun to give back? Giving enriches one's heart and soul—and it's contagious.

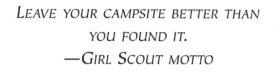

LEAVE YOUR CAMPSITE BETTER THAN YOU FOUND IT.
—GIRL SCOUT MOTTO

THE POINT OF GOOD WRITING IS KNOWING WHEN TO STOP.
—L. M. MONTGOMERY

CHAPTER TWELVE

THE BOTTOM LINE

Ethical values are child's play, not rocket science.

Society is forever fondly remembering the past as the "good old days," a warm, fuzzy recollection of the simpler, happier times of our youth. Nostalgia tends to be vague and selective. Truth be known, those times had their ups and downs, just like today, but, again, childhoods normally are less complex. Back then, we accepted plainspoken values and, for the most part, adhered to them. These norms were drilled into our heads by the adults who surrounded us. Their diligence influenced our behavior, just as we shaped the behavior of our children, and they of their offspring.

My intention in discussing these ageless values is to jog memories and to flip on light bulbs. There is little in this book that is original. Moral values are nothing new to any generation or culture.

These principles are ingrained in us from birth. Society's elders frequently view the younger generation as possessing fewer values than they have, but the fact is we all started the same. Each generation has unique challenges; no generation has a monopoly on values.

> *Society's elders frequently view the younger generation as possessing fewer values than they have, but the fact is we all started the same. Each generation has unique challenges; no generation has a monopoly on values.*

Although it may appear that the young people today are more inclined to cheat, they also are more tolerant of others than their parents. If they seem less inclined to paint morality in the stark blacks and whites, they also are less interested in making a million dollars and are more concerned about the condition of the earth 50 years from now. In sum and in retrospect, when it comes to values, each generation probably stacks up about even with the generation it succeeded and will precede it.

As an 18-year-old freshman at the University of Pennsylvania's Wharton School, I joined Sigma Chi. This fraternity was founded in 1855 when six students at Miami of Ohio University broke away from another fraternity over what they felt was improper behavior. As a Sigma Chi member, I pledged to uphold a credo of fairness, decency, and good manners.

I have never forgotten that promise. The "Jordan Standard," named for one of those six founders 150 years ago, insists each member, among other things, be of good and moral character and maintain the highest standards of honor and personal responsibility.

Such standards of proper behavior can be universally applied. No matter the faith, the culture, or the age, the natural goodness of human beings must be central to our dealings with one another.

There is an absolute requirement today to awaken in ourselves the basic values that help us determine right from wrong. I use the term *awaken* because our ethical values have been within us from the beginning, having been infused into our very beings by those who influenced us as youngsters.

We followed unwritten rules for the playgrounds and sandlots, homes, and schools. We honored basic fairness, decency, respect, and integrity. These principles do not change when we migrate from boxes full of sand to buildings full of desks. Then as today, we must conduct ourselves with honor and fairness.

> *These principles have not changed simply because we migrated from boxes full of sand to buildings full of desks.*

It's easy to keep a bargain or to honor a contract when it works in your favor. The measure of the individual is when his or her word is kept even when it puts the person at a disadvantage.

Tough times are never easy to manage. They often require a dramatic change of lifestyle. During a financial crisis, we must not only eliminate luxury and discretionary spending, we many times must curtail purchases of basic commodities—fuel, food, clothing. A planned purchase of a new house or car is back-burnered.

We must make do.

As a Jewish proverb points out, "He who can't endure the bad will not live to see the good." Financial setbacks usually pass. As another old saying goes, being poor is a state of mind; not having money is a temporary condition.

Notwithstanding the fact that a financial crisis can stretch ethical limits, for many others it can also push physical limits. For example, one ramification from financial worry is stress, a condition that can play havoc on the entire body. Stress walks hand in glove with financial worries. Hard times come in many forms and of varying durations. Some never seem to abate, stubbornly persisting, spreading heavy doses of sadness to all corners of our lives.

Take heart, philosophers tell us, for "this, too, shall pass away." At times, that doesn't seem possible, but try to remain positive and be surprised. Francis of Assisi told us: "Start by doing what is necessary, then what is possible, and suddenly you are doing the impossible."

As founder and chairman of the Huntsman Cancer Institute, I speak frequently with many cancer patients from around the world. I meet regularly with our staff of more than 1,600 scientists, researchers, clinicians, and staff members to discuss the disease and its ramifications. I have noticed that worry, stress, loneliness, and anxiety are key factors that not only have exacerbated cancer but often have prolonged the disease. On the other hand, joy, friendship, encouragement, and uplifting feelings have had a positive way of shortening cancer's duration and hastening remission.

When thinking of cancer, it helps to recall the soothing verse from Ecclesiastes: "To everything there is a season; a time for every purpose under heaven…. A time to weep and a time to laugh; a time to dance and a time to mourn." During episodes with cancer, it is, figuratively speaking, a time to laugh and a time figuratively to dance. It may seem odd, even impossible, but it helps body and spirit to try.

❖

Each human is unique. Each has unique ways in which to heal. Today's environment is conducive to stress in its many forms—anxiety, obsession, depression. Rising prices bring pressure to maintain certain lifestyles. Unemployment is up. Heath care is unaffordable. We frequently seem to be cash-strapped. More Americans are distraught today than at any time since the Great Depression.

Instead of moping about, we must turn this time into a period of positive reflection, a time for reaching out and helping others.

At the end of the day, isn't the real concern one of diminished status? And isn't it more a state of mind than a tangible situation? Assuming we have the basics—food, clothing, shelter—are we not still equipped to go forth and cheerfully help others?

Financial hardship is not the only fallout from bad times. Fear and turmoil are its silent partners. They can grip our soul and become personal hallmarks. They can make us consider doing things we might not otherwise entertain.

When we are fearful and submerged in chaos, we contemplate behavior not in keeping with our values. We, in turn, become fear and turmoil carriers, spreading havoc and heartache to those around us. (The Scrooge character in Dickens' *A Christmas Carol* makes the case. I believe we read and watch this story over and over, probably so it won't happen to us.)

Fear is bondage. I appreciate the well-established axiom because it is so true: We can unwittingly incarcerate ourselves with worry, negativity, and obsessive behavior. To do this is dangerous. It erodes health and spirit. It separates one from family, friends, and colleagues and destroys lasting relationships.

❖

In difficult and challenging times, we must embrace the many positive things in our lives, however small—children and loved ones, flowers and other beauties of nature, the gifts with which we are blessed. Over time, we see that most misfortunes are temporary situations that we perceive at the time as worst-possible scenarios but that turn out to be less permanent or severe than we had forecast.

So how does one bring about the restoration of value-based behavior in the marketplace and in the other arenas of modern life? I offer four simple suggestions, as follows:

- When you engage in something that affects others, first ask yourself: Is this right? Would I like to be treated this way?

- Take your values to work. Don't disconnect them when you sit down at your desk. There should not be a conflict between making a profit and adhering to traditional principles of decency and fairness.

- Consider yourself your brothers' and sisters' keeper and set the example for ethical behavior.

- Make the underpinnings of your life a string of f-words (phonetically, at least): family, faith, fortitude, fairness, fidelity, friendship, and philanthropy.

There should not be a conflict between making a profit and adhering to traditional principles of decency and fairness.

After family and faith, the most important of these attributes ought to be philanthropy. Most of us benefitted from a number of fortuitous breaks in life. Not one of us was truly self-made. We were helped or coached by others along the way. Thus, we have a special obligation to be on the lookout for opportunities to return those favors, or pass them on to others.

There are many causes out there awaiting our generosity. They come in all shapes and sizes. My own cause right now is finding a cure for cancer.

In considering which causes are the most worthwhile for us, look first to the needs in our communities. Put them in a priority that makes sense to you. Where can you do the most good? Where will our giving make a difference? Think it through and do our duty.

For me, the most exhilarating giving of all is based on a spur-of-the-moment impulse—taking the coat off your back for a shivering transient on a wintery street, or an unplanned drop-in at a homeless shelter. The impulse might even come in the middle of a speech, as happened to me a few years ago. I will close with that story.

Hanging on the wall behind my desk is a quote by John Andrew Holmes, a physician who authored *Wisdom in Small Doses*. It reads: "No exercise is better for the human heart than reaching down and lifting another up."

That powerful message was at the heart of a university commencement address delivered in 2000. It had to be the shortest graduation speech in modern history. Holmes' quote was the entire talk!

The commencement ceremony had been underway for nearly an hour and a half, and I had yet to give my prepared remarks. Family and friends were fidgeting in their seats; small children were fussing. The school was one that had a high proportion of older students, married students with families, students who worked full-time jobs for the opportunity to better their lives. They were a practical bunch; so were their parents and friends. Two hours of long-winded speakers was not their idea of a good use of time.

As I sat on the stage taking in all this, I began to mentally whittle my prepared text. By the time I approached the podium, I was down to a single sentence.

I stood before the graduates and asked them to stand. "Repeat after me," I instructed them. "No exercise … is better for the human heart … than reaching down … and lifting another up."

I asked them again to recite the 15-word thought.

Then, out of the blue, I did something completely on impulse. I turned to the school's president and announced that I would provide the university with 200 scholarships of $5,000 each. Then I sat down. You could have heard a pin drop in that events center. Mouths hung open, as if people questioned what they had heard. I could hardly believe what I had just said myself.

What followed was a deafening deluge of shouts, whistles, cheers, and applause. I was overwhelmed by the reaction.

As I absorbed the pandemonium, vivid memories of the long-ago Zellerbach Family Scholarship that made possible my degree from the University of Pennsylvania's Wharton School flashed before me. I even thought I could see Harold Zellerbach sitting there in the front row, quietly nodding and wearing one of those "we're even" smiles.

What a high! Try it. I guarantee you'll like it.

PERSPECTIVE

FROM LARRY KING

CNN

Jon Meade Huntsman may well be the most remarkable billionaire most of America has never heard of. Legendary in petrochemical circles, he operates around the globe in a quiet, determined, respected, and caring manner. For nearly two decades, he found himself in the upper tier of *Forbes* magazine's list of wealthiest Americans, but it wasn't always that way.

Jon is the embodiment of the American Dream. His was a journey from hardscrabble beginnings to chairman of America's largest family-owned and operated business. (In early 2005, he took the sprawling Huntsman empire public.)

As is the case with each Horatio Alger character, Jon Huntsman was afforded nothing but an
opportunity to compete on the field of dreams. The
rest—vision, determination, skill, integrity, a few
breaks, and ultimate success—was up to him.

He won that incredible race fair and square, ful-
filling his dream with moral principles intact, his
word being kept, dealing above board and fairly with
colleagues and competitors alike, and displaying a
demeanor of decency and generosity.

All this, to me, is the essence of Jon Huntsman.
It is why he has written this book and why it is
worth your time to read it.

His career was launched with an undergraduate
degree from the Wharton School at the University
of Pennsylvania, an education made possible by a
chance scholarship from someone who already had
it made. Jon went on to build an empire and render
an accounting for the favors and breaks he received
along the way.

You may not have heard of Jon Huntsman, but
the folks he has assisted over the years sure have.

Ask patients at the Huntsman Cancer Institute
and Hospital, a world-class research and patient

facility in Salt Lake City exploring how we might prevent and control the dreaded disease, especially hereditary cancers. The Huntsman family has given a quarter of a billion dollars so far to that effort and vows to double that amount in the coming years. Jon lost his mother, father, stepmother, and grand-parents to the disease. He himself has had cancer and beaten it. Twice.

Ask students and faculty at the Wharton School of Business at the University of Pennsylvania, where he became chairman of the Board of Overseers. His gift of $50 million made possible Huntsman Hall, a state-of-the-art business school complex, and the nation's leading international undergraduate program. Remembering what the chance for a college education meant to him, he has awarded several million dollars in scholarships over the years to employees' children and random students.

Ask the people of Armenia. Now there's a story worth telling.

On the evening of December 7, 1988, Jon and Karen Huntsman were watching the news in the living room of their striking Salt Lake City home. He was chief executive officer and chairman of Huntsman Chemical Corporation—an upstart in the stodgy and traditional chemical industry

The lead story on that nightly news was unsettling: An earthquake had devastated much of Armenia. Jon was riveted by the scenes of destruction unfolding before him: factories and apartments in rubble, roads and railways little more than twisted pretzels of concrete and steel, school buildings flattened, frantic survivors clawing through debris for loved ones.

A year earlier, Jon Huntsman probably could not have located Armenia on the map, but in the six previous months, he had negotiated with Aeroflot, the airline of the old Soviet government, to manufacture in a new Moscow plant plastic service ware for in-flight meals. In the process, he became the first American permitted to own a majority interest in a Soviet business. He had become fascinated with the USSR bear, and now disaster had struck one of its satellite states.

"We have to do something," he said to Karen that night. He was taking the suffering before him personally. That's how Jon Huntsman is.

The aid that followed ranged from expertise and resources for a modern cement factory that would produce concrete that could withstand most quakes to food and medical equipment to apartment complexes and schools—all as gifts to a grateful, battered nation.

Before he was finished 15 years later, the Huntsman family had infused $50 million of its money into Armenia, visiting the nation two dozen times. Yet, on that December 1988 night, he had no ties to that region of the world. He didn't know the name of a single victim. But the name Huntsman is not unknown in Armenia today, where Jon is an honorary citizen and recipient of the nation's highest award.

Who is Jon Huntsman? Ask those who have been helped. Ask the communities around the globe where Huntsman Corp. does business. They will tell of the deep, personal interest he has in their fortunes, their families, and their futures.

Perhaps that generosity is the residual of growing up on the other side of the economic tracks. If so, it is only part of his philanthropic equation. Jon also subscribes to the obligation of everyone to be generous. Throughout the ages, charity has been a cornerstone of most world cultures.

The Gospel of Giving according to Jon holds that every individual— whether financially stretched or of means, but especially the rich —is duty-bound to return a portion of his or her blessings.

Jon Huntsman is a different breed. He believes business is a creative endeavor, similar to a theater production, wherein integrity must be the central character. Notwithstanding what you hear on the nightly news or read in newspapers, decent *and* ethical behavior is not a moral heirloom of the past. He believes in being honest, fair, and gracious—even when it costs him several million dollars.

This book isn't simply a marketplace catechism for moral behavior. In every chapter, there are nuggets of good management techniques for those who run companies or organizations, solid instructions for those in mid-management, and a bigger picture for employees and memberships. With an MBA from the University of Southern California, Jon is not only an entrepreneur extraordinaire but also an experienced CEO who has seen it all.

For the past 35 years, his business has gone from scratch to annual revenues of $12 billion. It wasn't all smooth sailing. He was on the verge of bankruptcy twice, but his reputation for tough-but-fair negotiations, a gracious and sensitive demeanor, an entrepreneurial sense, and a remarkable philanthropic commitment give him a unique perspective from which to offer these rules of the road.

Jon Huntsman is living proof that you can do well by doing right. Leo Durocher was quite wrong when he said, "Nice guys finish last." Not only can nice people finish first, they finish better. Jon has little patience for situational ethics in the marketplace or life. He paints proper behavior in bold, black-and-white strokes. He believes in the adage that if you have one clock, everyone knows what time it is. If there are two, no one knows the precise time.

In 2002, I named him the Humanitarian of the Year because of his generosity to others. (*Business Week* ranks him among America's top philanthropists.) He even surprised me with a large, unexpected contribution to the Larry King Cardiac Foundation to help those who suffer from heart disease. My spouse, Shawn, and I count ourselves fortunate to have been friends of the Huntsman family for many years. I enthusiastically recommend his take on life.

PERSPECTIVE

FROM NEIL CAVUTO
MANAGING EDITOR,
FOX BUSINESS NETWORK

I know all about Jon Huntsman and the way he views life. I wrote the book on him.

In *More Than Money*, published in 2004, I featured Jon and some 20 other individuals who understand the value of meaning over money and, to me, represent the inspirational people of this world who continually turn personal challenges into a positive element of living. What you have just read is a basic blueprint of not only doing good but also being good.

Jon Huntsman's own life and personal values lend credence to his words. He walks his ethical talk and has done so in the face of incredible obstacles that at times surely must have made moral shortcuts tempting. Jon has no secret formula; it ought to be familiar to anyone with a conscience. But knowing what behavior is proper and what is not is the simple part. Living those principles requires commitment, integrity, and courage.

As a journalist and host of Fox News' *Your World*, cable TV's most-watched business show, I see it all. I, too, know of marketplace problems and of rotten apples in the business barrel, but in *Your World*, I attempt to go past the potholes. I go behind profit-and-loss ledgers to the individuals who make things happen.

In so doing, I have found many inspiring models who dispel the notion that what's good for business can't be good for me; men and women who are catalysts for wondrous endeavors, who know not only how to play by the rules but embrace ethical conduct. Genuinely successful business executives know there can be no dissonance between society's values and corporate operations.

In my book, *More Than Money*, I define those who have gained fame and fortune not so much by their achievements as by how they got there—the enormous odds they overcame, the dignity and courage they displayed in the process, the way they treated people ethically and fairly along the way.

These heroes learned to train their eyes on the possibilities, not the odds. They made bumps in the road to success fodder for motivation—a motivation, incidentally, that is not solely centered on profits and power but also on making a difference in the lives of others.

A born philanthropist and self-made multibillionaire, Jon Huntsman is a textbook example of what I am talking about. Notably, he turned personal cancer setbacks—holding his mother at her death, watching his father waste away, being informed one year to the day that doctors told him he had prostate cancer that he now had an unrelated cancer—into a beacon of hope for others who find themselves with this dreaded affliction.

With nearly a quarter of a billion dollars of personal funds as seed money, and the promise of more where that came from, Jon launched a cancer research institute a decade ago and followed up with an accompanying research hospital seven years later. Together, they are the centerpiece of his search for controlling, if not curing, cancer.

The Huntsman Cancer Institute and Hospital is a scientifically and architecturally stunning complex.

The research into identifying inherited cancer genes and controlling the disease with early intervention is breathtaking. The hospital has the patient's comfort and dignity foremost in mind. It reminds you of a four-star hotel rather than a place where sick people are housed. And it is about to double in size.

Given my own experience with cancer, I am in awe of Jon's indefatigable crusade to conquer this insidious disease. He shakes down pharmaceutical companies, federal agencies, and wealthy colleagues; makes political donations to Republicans and Democratic members of Congress who vote for cancer-fighting appropriations; and personally visits patients undergoing chemotherapy. When the chemical industry took a nosedive in 2001, he took out a multimillion-dollar personal loan to cover his philanthropic pledges until the bottom line rebounded three years later. He took his family-owned petrochemical empire public in early 2005, in part, to raise additional hundreds of millions for his cancer institute.

(Incidentally, Jon is routing his royalties from this book to the Institute, and I know he would most gratefully accept additional donations. The address, should you be so inclined, is: Huntsman Cancer Institute, 2000 Circle of Hope, Salt Lake City, UT 84112.)

In Jon Huntsman's world, giving is a sacred duty. He doesn't think much of billionaires who wait until they are dead to give away their money. I sometimes think Jon would be happiest if he could coincide his final breath with giving away his last dollar to someone in need, thus allowing him to leave this world the way he entered it.

But the thrust of *More Than Money* went well beyond identifying philanthropic stars. My heroes are those who squarely faced life's hurdles, overcame them, and did so with class, high principle, and a sense of decency.

Thanks to *Winners Never Cheat*, we have been reintroduced to our values roadmap. It gives each of us simple directions on how to become a hero.

PERSPECTIVE

FROM WAYNE REAUD

TRIAL ATTORNEY

I'm a trial lawyer, and this book could put me out of business. Nobody would be happier about it than me.

Over the past 30 years, I have taken some of America's biggest corporations to court, calling them to task for behavior that threatened people's health and livelihoods. From asbestos makers to tobacco purveyors to computer manufacturers, I have fought to make big companies more account-able in their business dealings.

Ordinarily, you would not expect a trial lawyer to be particularly close with the CEO of a big cor-poration. So when people hear that Jon Huntsman and I are good friends, and have been for 15 years, they tend to scratch their heads. In the ecology of the business world, aren't we natural enemies? Don't our respective jobs put us at odds with each other? The answer to both questions is no. And the reason is simple: Jon Huntsman is not your average CEO.

Jon is a true rarity in the corporate world: a hugely successful entrepreneur whose conscience is as sharp as his business sense, whose word is known as an unbreakable bond. From his very first job, picking potatoes in rural Idaho at age eight, to his current position of running one of the world's largest chemical companies, he has always put ethical concerns on equal, if not greater, footing than his business concerns.

I could give you a laundry list of things Jon has done—donating record-setting amounts to cancer treatment and research, tithing to his church, giving millions to colleges and universities—but that still wouldn't give you a clear idea of why he's so unusual. His ethics go far deeper than simply making donations and glad-handing for good causes. They are at the core of his being. They are, for him, a way of life.

In Plato's seminal work, *The Republic*, he gives us the notion of the ideal leader: the "philosopher-king." This is the man who possesses the perfect marriage of a philosophic mind and an ability to lead. As Plato wrote: "I need no longer hesitate to say that we must make our guardians philosophers. The necessary combination of qualities is extremely rare. Our test must be thorough, for the soul must be trained up by the pursuit of all kinds of knowledge to the capacity for the pursuit of the highest—higher than justice and wisdom—the idea of the good."

Jon Huntsman has pursued "the idea of the good" all his life and, as his corporate track record underscores, he's more than able to lead. But the true test of ethics comes not when a person gives with nothing to lose. It comes when he gives with everything to lose. That's why Jon Huntsman is the right man to do this book. And there's no question that he's doing it at just the right time. In this age of Enron, Tyco, insider-trading scandals, and rampant corporate malfeasance, we need Jon Huntsman's voice and leadership more than ever.

I hope Jon's book will remind us all that, like him, you can do well and do good at the same time.

As a trial lawyer, I want every businessperson in America to read this book and take to heart Jon's example. Maybe then my fellow trial lawyers and I would have nothing left to do.

There's nothing I'd like better.